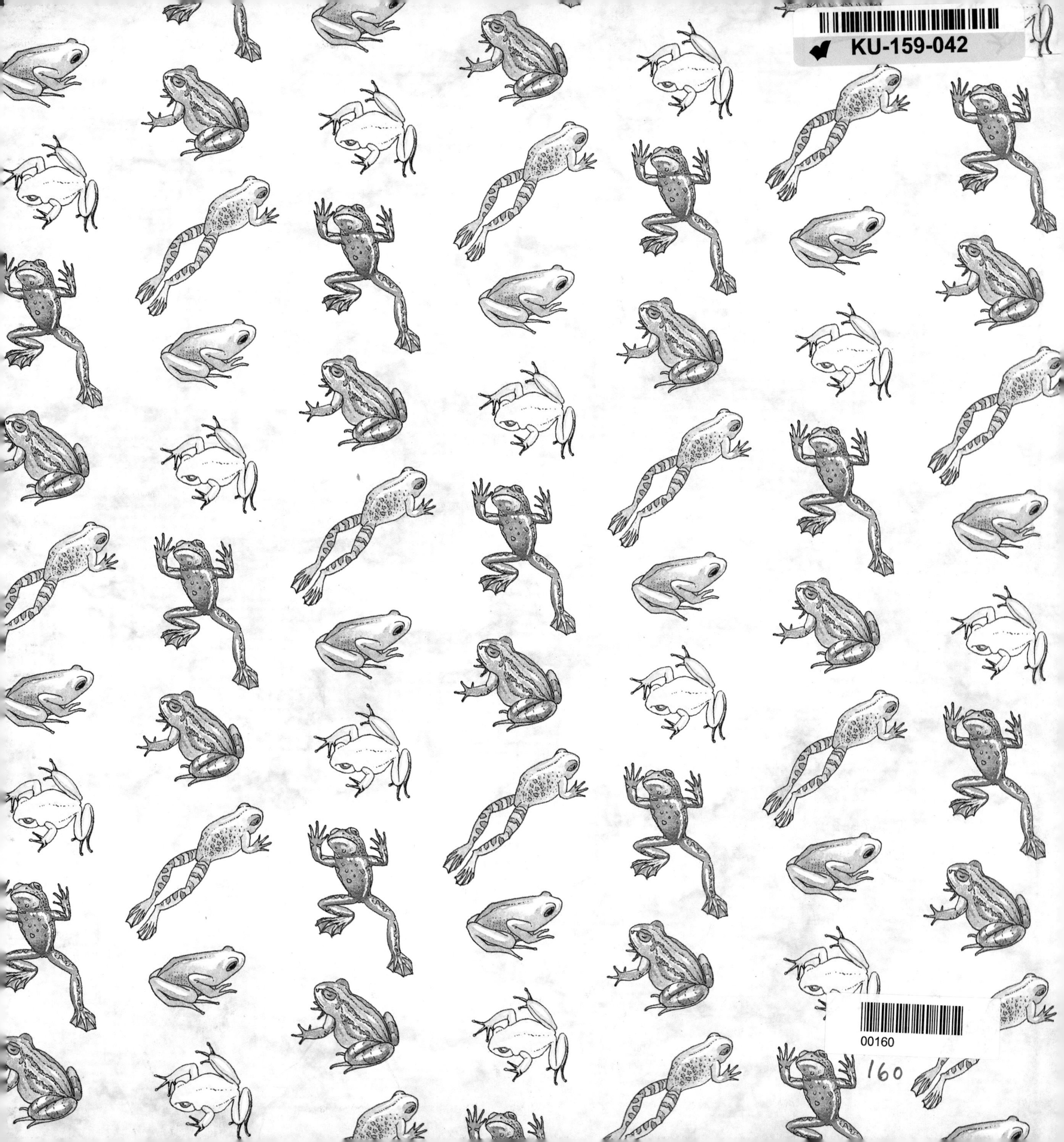

INSIGHTS

FROGS AND TOADS

STEVE PARKER

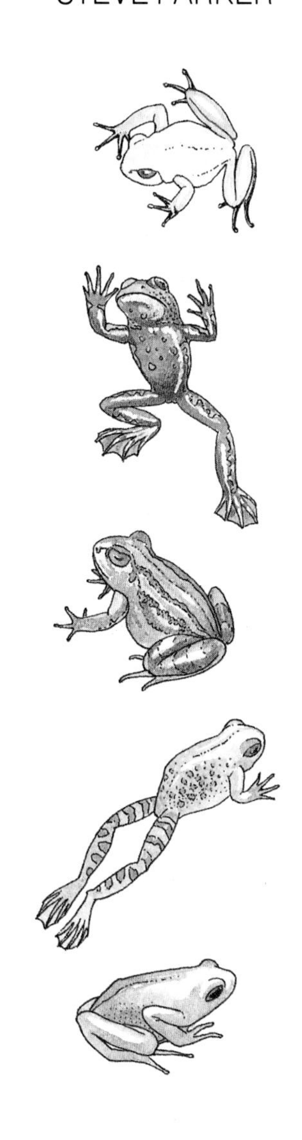

INSIGHTS

FROGS AND TOADS

STEVE PARKER

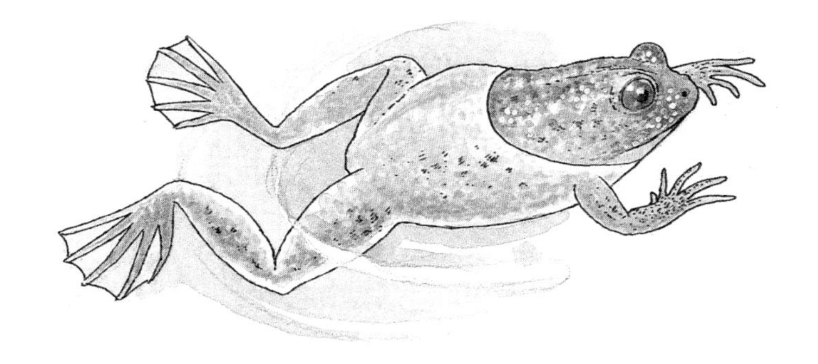

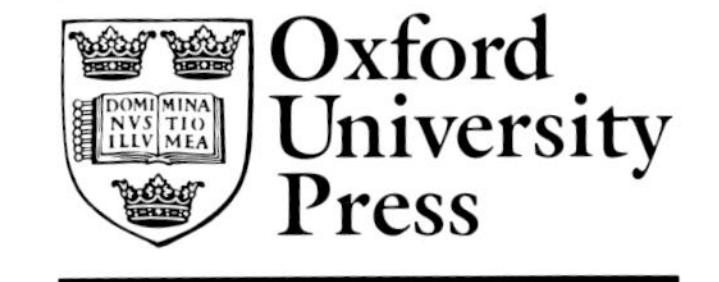

A QUARTO BOOK

Published by
Oxford University Press, Walton Street, Oxford, OX2 6DP
Oxford New York Toronto Delhi Bombay Calcutta Madras Karachi
Petaling Jaya Singapore Hong Kong Tokyo Nairobi Dar Es Salaam Cape Town

and associated companies in Berlin Ibadan

Oxford is a trade mark of Oxford University Press

A catalogue record for this book is available from the British Library.

ISBN 0 19 910040 3

This book was designed and produced by
Quarto Publishing plc
The Old Brewery, 6 Blundell Street, London N7 9BH

Series Editor (Natural History) Steve Parker

Art Director Nick Buzzard
Publishing Director Janet Slingsby

Senior Editor Paul Szuscikiewicz
Copy Editor Susan Berry
Designer John Grain
Illustrators Paul Richardson, Ann Savage
Picture Manager Sarah Risley

The Publishers would like to thank the following for their help in the preparation of this book: Penny Dawes, Trish Going, Dave Kemp, Constance Novis, Katie Preston.

Picture Acknowledgements Key: a = above, b = below, l = left, r = right, c = centre
Quarto Publishing would like to thank Heather Angel's Picture Library – Biofotos – for supplying the majority of pictures for this book, all of which were taken by her except Brian Rogers, pages 12r, 17r, 20c, b, 26, 27, 42b, 43al, b, 45a. Additional pictures by: Bruce Davidson/Survival Anglia, page 32; Wildlife Matters, page 45b.
While every effort has been made to trace and acknowledge all copyright holders, we would like to apologize should any omissions have been made.

Typeset by Central Southern Typesetters, Eastbourne, East Sussex
Manufactured in Hong Kong by Regent Publishing Services Ltd
Printed in Hong Kong by Leefung-Asco Printers Ltd

CONTENTS

What are Frogs and Toads?

Damp and slimy, dry and warty, poisonous and skulking, pop-eyed and cute – frogs are many things to many people. Few other animals are the subject of so many legends and folk tales – most of which are untrue! Yet the truth about frogs and toads is stranger still. These fascinating creatures are members of the amphibian group – in other words they can live on land and in water. They are all hunters, catching animals to eat. And they live all over the world, except in the seas and in the cold near the North and South poles.

There are nearly 3,500 kinds, or species, of frogs and toads around the world. Some are smaller than your thumbnail, while a few would fill a dinner plate. But most of them are less than 5 cm (2 in) long, and live in warm, wet places, such as tropical rainforests and marshes. They need dampness

▲ **Frog meets toad**
A bright-coloured, smooth-skinned European frog (on the left) comes face to face with a dull, dry, warty European toad. A fight is unlikely, since they live in different places and rarely meet in nature.

THE FIRST FROGS

Fossils, the remains of animals preserved in the rocks, tell us that amphibians first appeared on the Earth about 360 million years ago. They had developed from fish, over millions of years of evolution. Early amphibians such as *Ichthyostega* were like large lungfish, with legs and even a few scales. The first frogs, such as *Vieraella*, swam in prehistoric ponds 170 million years ago.

▲ *Ichthyostega* was about 1 m (3 ft) long, including its tail.

▲ *Vieraella*, an early frog, lived alongside the dinosaurs.

▲ The fire salamander, from Europe, comes out at night.

OTHER AMPHIBIANS

Besides frogs and toads, there are two other main groups of amphibians. One is the newts and salamanders, with about 360 different kinds, or species. They are similar to frogs, but their bodies are longer and thinner, and they have long tails. The other group is the strange caecilians. There are about 160 kinds, and most of them burrow in the soils of tropical jungles. They have no legs, and they look like worms. But they are fierce hunters of real worms, insects and other soil creatures. The biggest grow to more than 60 cm (23½ in) long and can give you a powerful bite.

▲ This great crested newt is laying an egg on a pond leaf.

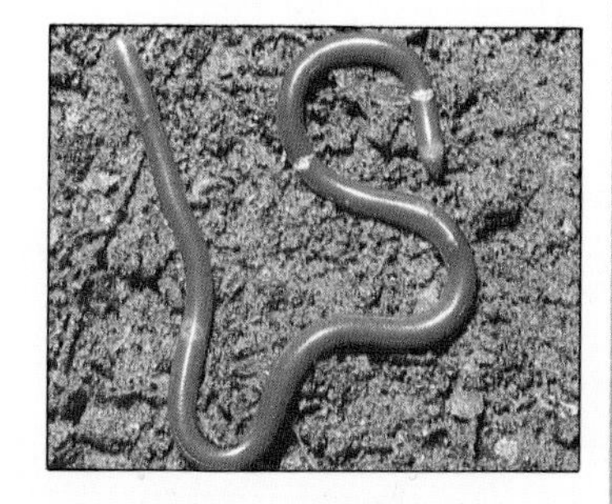

▲ A caecilian from the tropics, ready to burrow underground.

▼ **"Flying" frog**
The Costa Rican flying frog glides 15 m (50 ft) on huge webbed feet.

because their skin is not fully waterproof, and their body fluids would dry out in warm, dry conditions. Also, frogs and toads breathe partly through their skin. They have lungs, like us, but they must also take in oxygen from the air around them. They can only do this through moist skin.

A few frogs and toads even live in dry deserts and scrubland. During the day, they hide from the sun's heat in burrows or under logs and stones. They come out only during the cool and damp of night-time.

Frog or toad?

All frogs and toads are amphibians,as are their cousins, the newts and salamanders. Although we think of frogs as different from toads there is no real distinction.

Ponds and streams
Each type of frog has its own habitat. The European marsh frog (above) spends most of its life in swampy ponds, streams, and ditches. The northern cricket frog from North America (below) likes still, shallow water with damp vegetation nearby.

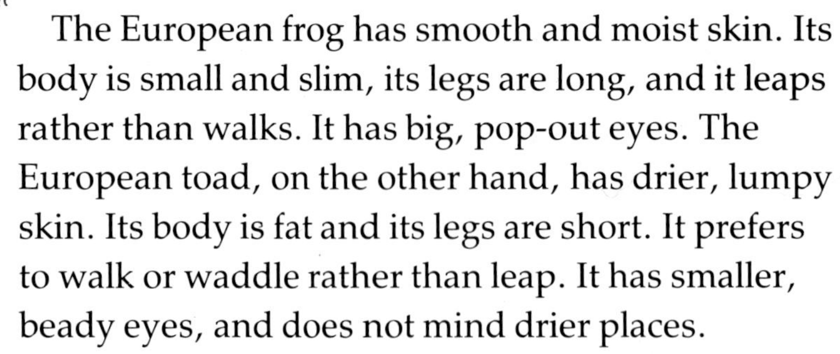

The European frog has smooth and moist skin. Its body is small and slim, its legs are long, and it leaps rather than walks. It has big, pop-out eyes. The European toad, on the other hand, has drier, lumpy skin. Its body is fat and its legs are short. It prefers to walk or waddle rather than leap. It has smaller, beady eyes, and does not mind drier places.

But in other regions, the differences are much less clear. What one person calls a frog, another may call a toad. There is not one scientific group for frogs and another for toads. They are all in the same group, *Anura,* meaning "tail-less". And this is how they differ from newts and salamanders, which have tails.

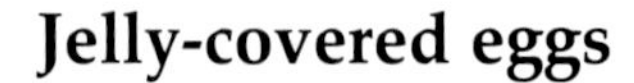

Jelly-covered eggs

Frogs, toads, and all other amphibians lay jelly-covered eggs, called spawn. These are usually laid in water. They hatch into tadpoles which can breathe underwater, using gills (see page 24). Frogs and toads in the desert wait until a rainstorm forms puddles, then they lay their eggs in these.

As a tadpole grows, it goes through an amazing transformation. Its tail and gills shrink, and its legs grow. Gradually it changes into the adult frog-like shape. However, it does not begin living out of the water, on land, until it finally loses its tail. These two features – jelly-covered spawn and tadpoles that gradually change into grown-up adults – make amphibians different from any other animal group.

Tropics
The red-eyed tree frog (above) of Central America is one of many tree frogs that rarely come down to the ground. The Surinam toad (below), from South America, likes slow rivers.

Mountains

The tiny Seychelles frog, less than 3 cm (1 in) long, lives on the tropical islands of the same name in the Indian Ocean. Not a good climber, it stays hidden in the mossy undergrowth of mountainside forests. Like many other frogs, it is very rare and needs our protection.

Deserts

The red-spotted toad is quite at home with the cacti and sagebrush of the North America desert. It avoids the heat of the day, and comes out at night to prey on crickets, beetles, and other small creatures. It only ventures out by day when there has been a rare rainstorm.

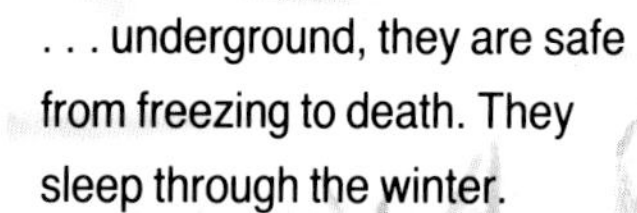

. . . underground, they are safe from freezing to death. They sleep through the winter.

▲ Arum frog

This 6 cm (2 in) frog from South Africa is so named because the male often climbs onto an arum lilly plant to sing his courting song to the female. Many frogs get their names from the type of habitat they are in, or the vegetation they are on, when people notice them and study them.

▼ White's tree frog

This large, dumpy tree frog thrives in many places in its homeland of Australia. It has tough skin, through which water passes less easily, so it does not lose its body fluids and become dehydrated in dry regions. White's tree frog is very adaptable and lives in scrubland, woods, and around houses too, hiding in outbuildings and even letterboxes!

▲ Forests and woods
Frogs and toads have mainly secret lives, although we may notice them at breeding time, when they croak and call, and splash about in the water as they mate. For the rest of the year, they usually leave their breeding ponds and streams to sit among damp plants, or under logs and stones, waiting for food.

WHERE DO FROGS GO IN THE WINTER?
In warm tropical regions, frogs and toads can be active all year round. In places with cold winters, their bodies cool down and they cannot move. So, before the frosts and snows arrive, they dig into loose soil among tree roots or under hedges, and . . .

FROG FEATURES

The typical frog is a neckless, small-bodied, wide-mouthed, long-legged leaper. It has tiny teeth and cannot bite properly, so its mouth must be big enough to gulp down prey whole. Its back legs are enormously long and strong for take-off when leaping, and its front legs act as shock-absorbers for landing. For much of its time, a frog quietly waits for prey.

Even frogs and toads that live in water only during the breeding season are well designed for a watery life. A frog's eyes and nostrils are on the very top of its head. So when it is lying almost under the water, it can still see and breathe and smell.

The overall shape of a frog gives clues to its lifestyle. Those with a slender body, a pointed nose, and long legs with big webbed feet probably spend a lot of time in the water. The streamlined

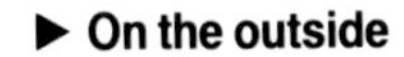

▶ On the outside
Most of the frog's body is covered with thin, moist skin. This produces a layer of slippery mucus (slime). The mucus helps to stop the skin drying out, and makes it difficult for a predator to hold the frog. Frogs shed their skin and grow a new one regularly. Some even eat the old skin, to recycle the nutrients. The skin also has poison glands, as shown opposite.

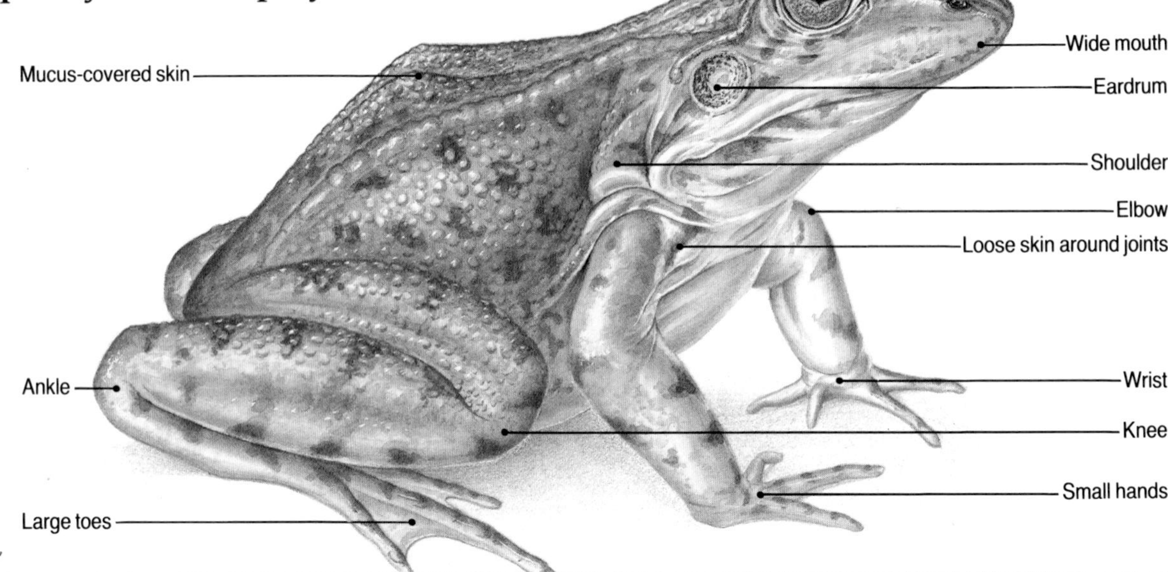

Digging feet

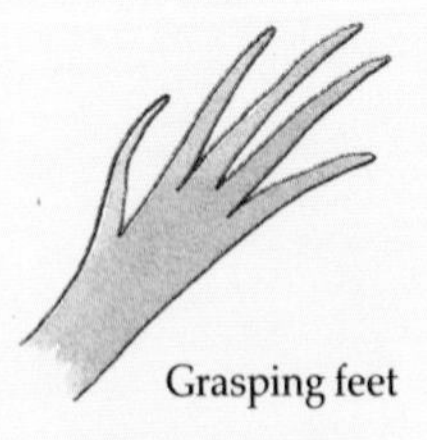

Grasping feet

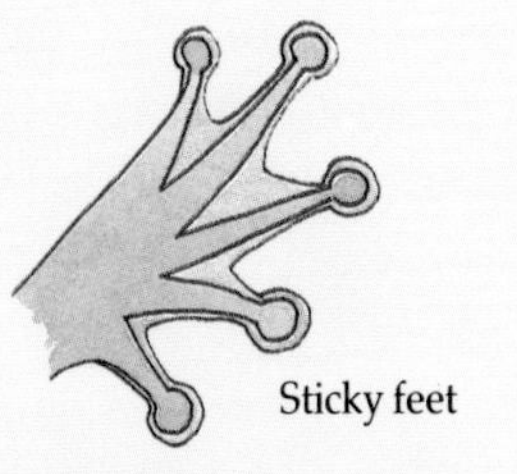

Sticky feet

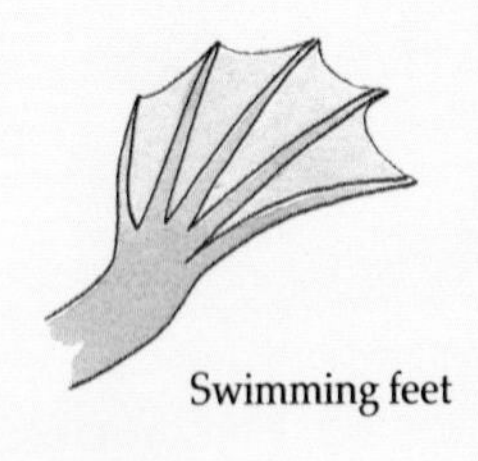

Swimming feet

FROG FEET

A frog's feet show where and how it lives. Wide, spade-like feet with knobs and strong joints usually mean it spends a lot of time digging and burrowing, like the spadefoot toad. Long, slender toes can wrap around plant stems, when the frog is climbing among the reeds. Tree frogs have fingertip discs with sticky pads, which can grip even the shiniest leaf. Webs of skin between the toes mean the frog is a powerful swimmer. It spreads its toes and pushes against the water to propel itself forward.

shape helps speedy swimming and diving.

Those with a flattened body and large discs on their fingertips are probably tree frogs as they can balance more easily if they have a low, flat body. Some tree frogs can even walk up windows with their sticky toes.

Those with a wide body and short, stumpy legs are likely to be land-dwelling frogs, which creep under rocks and hide under logs.

▲ Big eyes
Frogs hunt mainly by sight. Their large eyes can see well by day and at night. Special "bug detectors" inside the eyes pick out small moving objects. This is a forest tree frog from Africa.

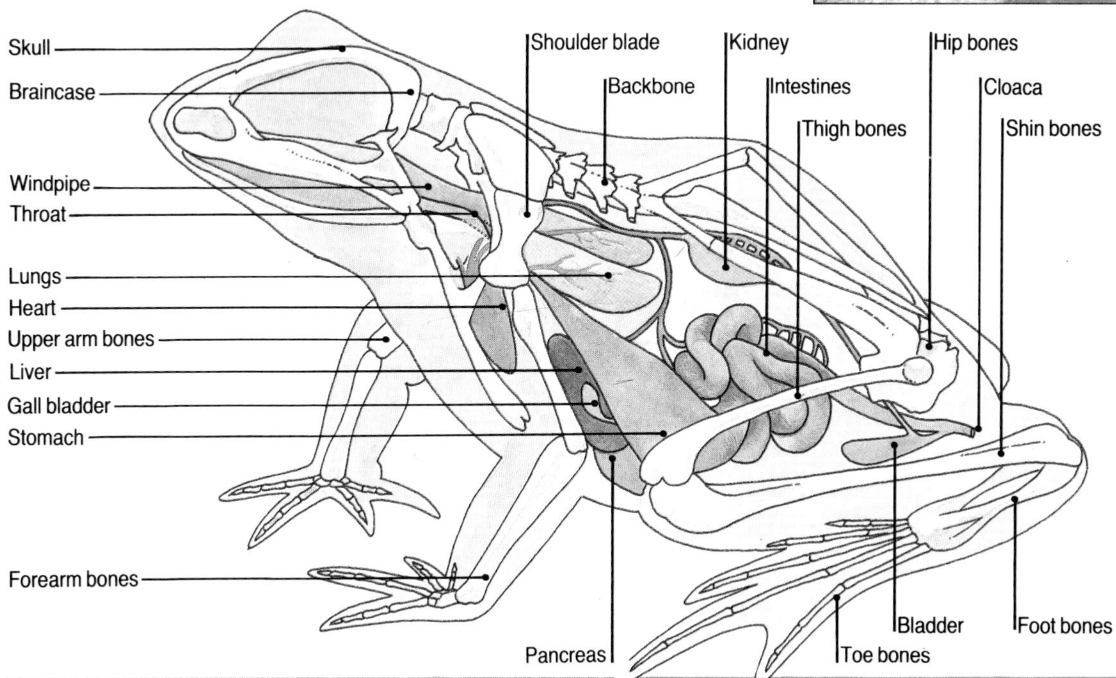

◀ On the inside
The frog has a bony skeleton like us. But compared with us its backbone is very short and thick, while its hip and leg bones are huge.

SLIME AND POISON

The skin of a frog or toad makes mucus, and in many species it makes poison, too. The microscopic poison and mucus glands are dotted over the skin. There is also a large poison gland behind each ear, the parotid gland, which oozes horrible liquid when the frog is threatened.

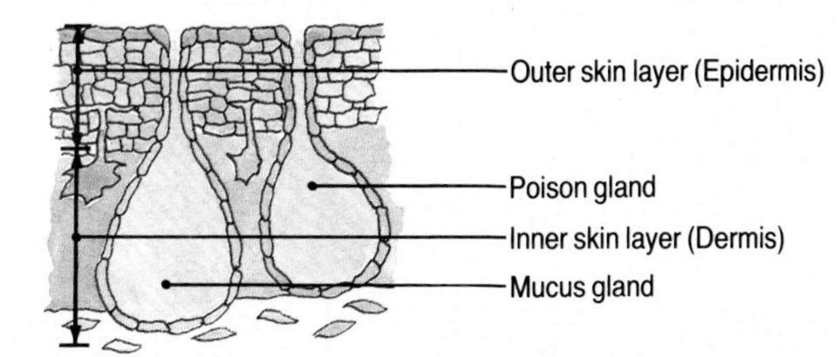

▲ A diagram of frog skin. In real life, the skin is only about 1 mm (0.04 in) thick.

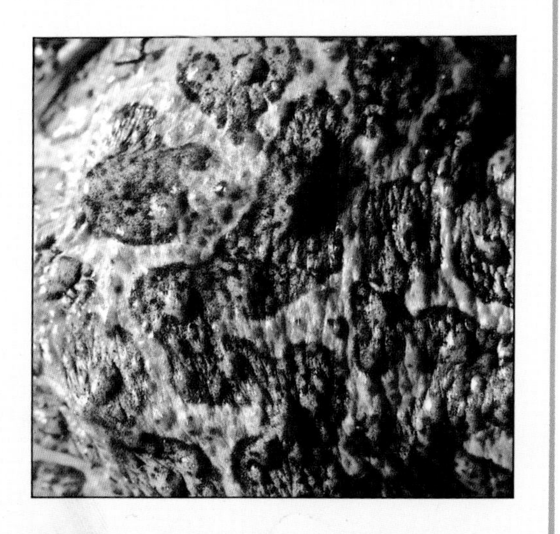

▶ The warty, knobbly skin of a green toad, shown three times larger than life-sized.

Frog Colours

In spring-time at a marsh or pond, frogs croak noisily to each other. But can you spot them in the waterweeds? Their colours and patterns blend well with the surroundings – this is called camouflage. See if you can find five camouflaged frogs on the left. Other frogs, brilliantly coloured in blues, reds, and oranges, warn you not to touch.

◀ Piece of bark
This grey tree frog from North America looks just like flaky bark mottled with lichens and mosses. But it must stay still, or its disguise will be ruined.

▶ Folded leaf
The tiny leaf-folding frog lives in tropical Ecuador. It wriggles into a groove in a leaf and hangs onto the smooth surface with its sticky fingertips.

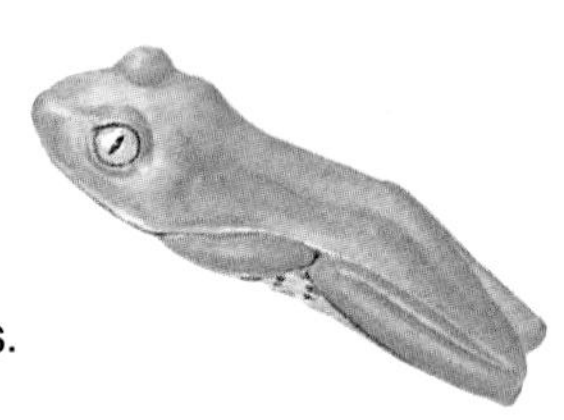

◀ Speckly leaf-blade
Another frog from Ecuador, South America, the speckled tree frog, has a pattern of faint spots over its back. It crouches down so that its pale underside does not show.

▼ Crinkly old leaf
The amazing casque-headed frog is another Ecuador inhabitant. Its strange pointed head and spotty colours exactly match the shape and colour of the old leaves where it hides.

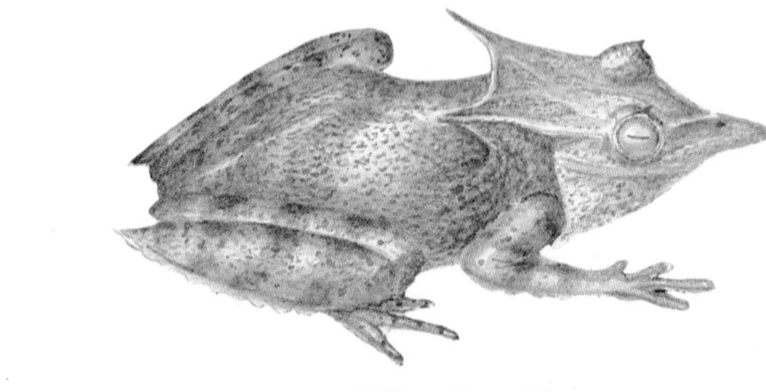

◀ Bits of forest floor
The pale strip down the body of this Malaysian striped wood frog, helps to break up the usual frog outline, making it harder to see.

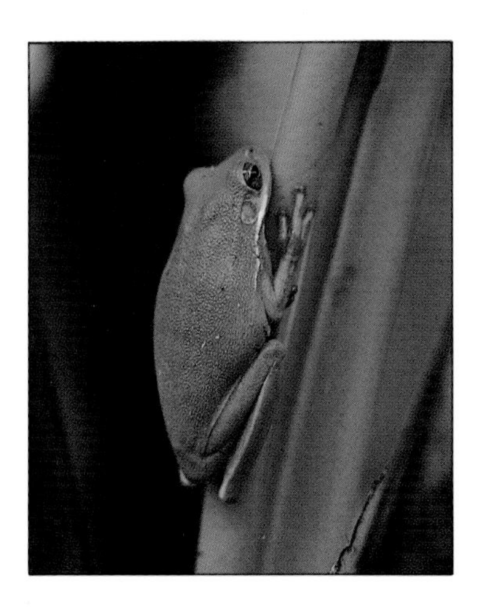

◀ **A greeny bulge**
A vital part of camouflage is the ability to sit still. Predators would probably not notice this American green tree frog, if it does not move.

▼ **Part of the streamside**
Damp boulders on stream banks are often covered with patchy mosses and lichens. The lichen stream frog from Central America merges with its background.

Frogs and toads come in almost every colour under the sun, from jet-black to near-white. Some are the same colour all over, others have dazzling sets of spots, blotches, zig-zags and stripes. Why is there so much colour and variety in the frog world?

Over millions of years of evolution, each kind of frog and toad has become exactly suited to surviving in its natural surroundings. Skin colour is part of evolution, and it helps in two ways. One is to do with secrecy, and concealing, another with being obvious, and advertising.

Camouflage for concealment

Being well camouflaged means you are less likely to be detected. Camouflage is doubly useful for a frog or toad. First, it helps the frog to avoid becoming a meal. It is difficult for a predator like a snake to see a frog that is coloured like a patch of waterweed, hiding among the waterweed.

Second, camouflage helps when the frog, in its turn, is the predator – to catch a meal. Good camouflage means a victim is less likely to notice you. Most frogs and toads ambush their prey. They

▶ **Who eats old bark?**
Few predators are interested in a scrap of bark. So in camouflage, it helps to look like something which is difficult to eat and has little nourishment. But this scrap of bark is really Bransford's frog, from Central America.

◀ **Waiting and hoping**
A South American horned toad stays still and waits for an insect, a small rodent such as a mouse, or even another frog. It must succeed at the first lunge, since it is too slow to give chase.

▲ Red for danger
A tiny arrow-poison frog from Central and South America has enough poison to kill you! These frogs got their name because jungle tribes tipped their hunting arrows and darts with the poison.

► Corroboree cheat
Bright yellow-and-black stripes make the corroboree frog from Australia look highly poisonous, but it is actually harmless. In nature, pretending to be poisonous in this way is called mimicry.

▲ Wasp of the frog world
Yellow-and-black stripes are a common warning pattern in nature. They are shared by bees and wasps, some venomous snakes, and this arrow-poison frog from South America.

hide quietly, hardly moving, and then wait for a small creature to pass by. As it does, the frog flicks out a long tongue or jumps forward and snaps at the prey.

Shape and behaviour

Many tree frogs are a plain glossy green, to match the shiny leaves where they hide. Woodland frogs are often mottled brown, to merge in with bark, twigs and old leaves. Reed-dwellers have stripy blotches, like plant stems.

Body size and shape are important to camouflage, too; so is behaviour. If a tree frog senses danger, it may squat down and keep very still. Squatting makes its body even more leaf-shaped, and lack of movement makes it hard to spot. Frogs waiting for prey also keep still as part of their ambush tactics.

Advertisement : a health warning!

What about frogs and toads with bright colours and busy movements? They look a bit like an advertisement, as though they want to be noticed.

Most frogs and toads make some sort of horrible-tasting or poisonous fluid in their skin glands. Those with bright red, orange and blue coloured bodies usually have very powerful poisons that would kill any animal which tried to eat them. Their colours act as a warning, in the same way that a red "Accident" sign on the highway warns motorists of danger ahead. Predators soon learn that a frog with bright colours is foul-tasting or poisonous, and they avoid similar frogs in future. This way, the frog is protected by its brilliance.

▲ Flashy markings
The vlei frog of South Africa has a surprise up its sleeve, or rather under its legs. If a predator comes too close, it kicks open its legs to reveal bright red stripes. Then it leaps away, lands, and quickly folds its legs again to hide the red colour. The predator is surprised by the sudden stripes – and by their mysterious disappearance!

FRIGHTFUL EYES

A few frogs and toads have eye-spot markings near their back legs. If threatened, they turn their back to the enemy and raise their puffed-up bodies. Large, frightening "eyes" appear, that look as though they belong to a cat, hawk or owl. The enemy is surprised, and the frog escapes.

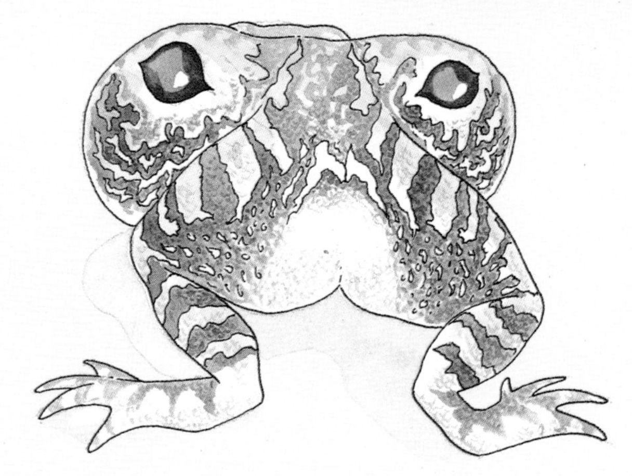

BEING BIG AND FIERCE

If a toad or frog has to face its attacker, it may try to look as big and fierce as possible. It puffs itself up, stands tall, and hisses loudly. Snakes, in particular, have to swallow their prey whole (they cannot chew), so they may be put off by such a large, noisy prey.

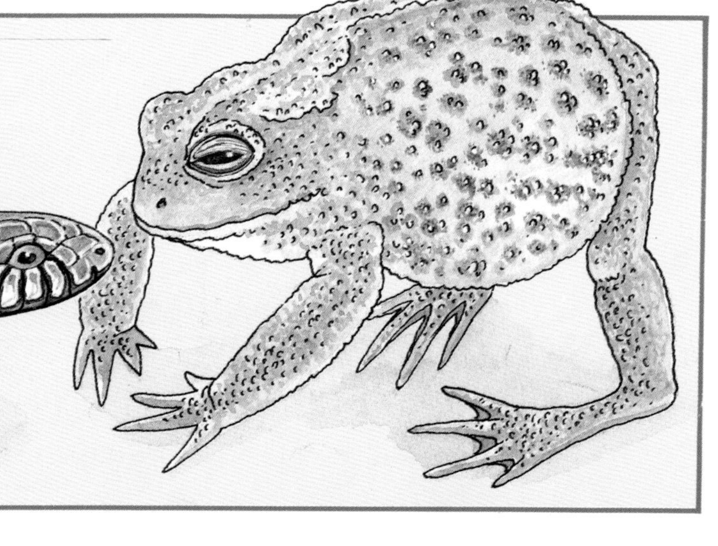

GETTING TOGETHER

One of the most fascinating parts of frog life is their croaky courtship. At the start of the breeding season, frogs and toads make their way to traditional breeding places such as ponds, swamps and slow-flowing rivers. The males start to sing to the females in an incredible chorus of croaks, clicks, buzzes, squeaks and grunts. Sometimes the noise is so loud at the breeding pool, you can hardly hear yourself speak. The females are attracted by this frog chorus and then the males and females pair up and are ready to breed.

▲ Singing in the dark
As the male painted reed frog sings, his chin swells up with air and becomes bigger than his body! Like many small frogs, he calls at dusk and at night. He's less at risk from predators under the cover of darkness.

◄ Peeping in spring
The spring peeper is a little frog, only 3 cm (1.1 in) long, common in North America. Its pure whistling call sounds like a penny flute or high-pitched continuous ringing. When it is heard, it means that spring is on the way. The males climb up into branches above the water, and sing their "peep-peep-peep" song to the females. Each "peep" lasts only about one-third of a second.

▲ A balloon for a chin
In the damp woods of tropical Central America, you probably would not spot the foam-nest frog hiding under leaves. But you would certainly hear it at breeding time. The male attracts a female by loud calls, as his thin, flexible chin swells with air like a rubber balloon (see opposite). The female lays her eggs in a nest of bubbles and mucus foam whipped up in a puddle.

▼ Is there anyone there?
Deep in the forest of Papua New Guinea, South-East Asia, a tiny microhylid frog squeaks for a mate. By day it crouches on the branches, easily confused with a knotty piece of twig!

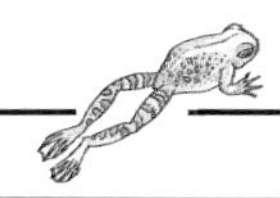

Frogs and toads, like other amphibians, need water at the breeding season – to lay their eggs in. A few frogs and toads bring up their tadpoles in unusual places but most lay their eggs in water – whether it's a huge lake or a tiny puddle.

Before the female frog lays her eggs, she must find a male frog, who will fertilize the eggs with his sperm. If he does not, the eggs will not develop into tadpoles. For most of the year, frogs and toads live alone but in order to breed they must get together.

Signs from the surroundings

As the climate changes, the breeding season approaches. Female frogs develop eggs in their bodies, and males make their sperm.

In tropical places, frogs get ready to breed as the rainy season starts, when pools and puddles form. In places such as Europe and North America, they get ready in spring, as the days become warmer and longer. Ponds and marshes thaw, and food becomes plentiful.

Each frog and toad usually makes its way to the place where it was born. Breeding sites are

TWO FROM ONE

All frogs that look like this one were once put in the same species – the grey tree frog, *Hyla versicolor*. But when scientists recorded and analyzed their calls, they discovered that what they thought was one species was really two. Some of the frogs had a different call and these are now known as *Hyla chrysoscelis*.

▼ This is a real grey tree frog (*Hyla versicolor*).

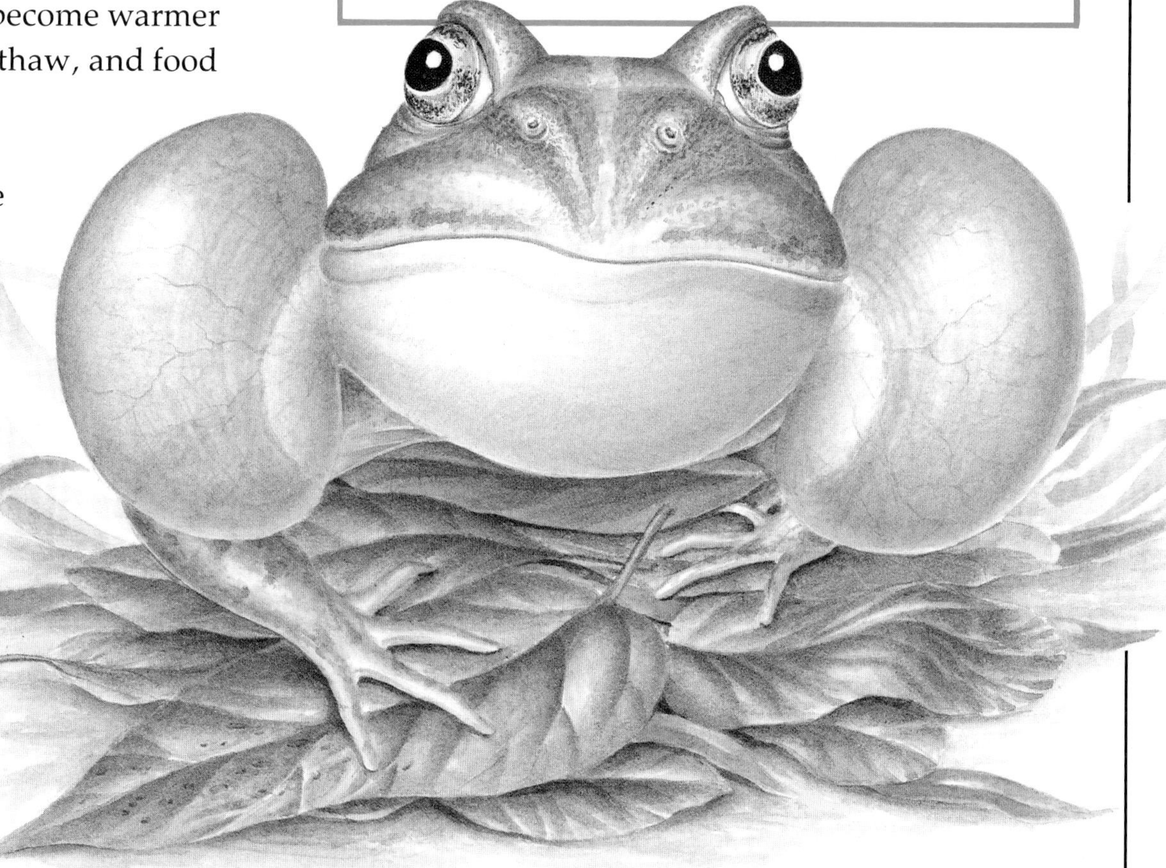

▶ **What a cheek!**
Frogs and toads make their calls using their vocal cords, in the same way that you sing. But a frog breathes in, then closes its mouth, and moves the air quickly to and fro between the lungs in its chest, and the space in its mouth. As air goes into the closed mouth it makes special patches of thin skin, known as vocal sacs, blow up like balloons. Some frogs have vocal sacs in their chins. Others have them in the cheeks, as shown here.

used year after year (unless they have been filled in or destroyed by people). They are soon alive with toads and frogs, waddling and hopping towards the water.

Frog chorus

The noisiest event in the frog's year is its courtship. Each species has its own call, from the croaks and grunts of common species, to grunts, trills, pops and whistles, even a buzzing sound like a chainsaw. Some frogs are named after their calls, such as the bullfrog, the bell frog, and the barking tree frog.

Usually the males make the calls, which have several purposes. One is to guide the females to the

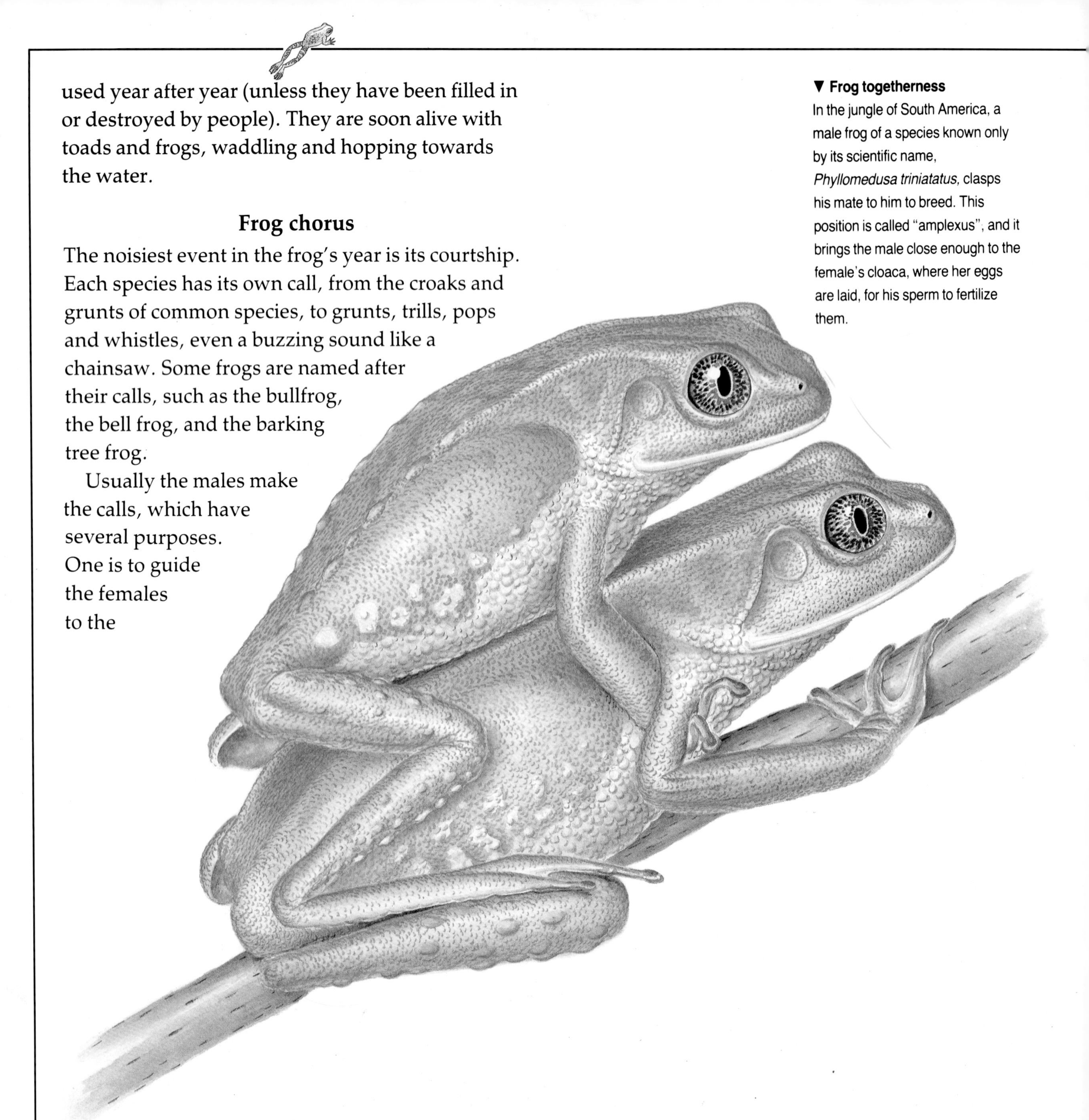

▼ Frog togetherness
In the jungle of South America, a male frog of a species known only by its scientific name, *Phyllomedusa triniatatus*, clasps his mate to him to breed. This position is called "amplexus", and it brings the male close enough to the female's cloaca, where her eggs are laid, for his sperm to fertilize them.

FROG WITH A TAIL

Although frogs do not have proper tails, with backbones inside them, some look as though they do. This one is called, sensibly enough, the tailed frog. Only the male has the soft, fleshy "tail". He uses it to place his sperm inside the female's body. This means the eggs are fertilized before they are laid. A few frogs that mate on land, not in the water, also have "tails" like this.

breeding place. Another is to make sure a female gets together with a male from her own species. The water may be writhing with dozens of frog species, and she chooses her mate by sound as well as sight. Yet another purpose is to ensure that the male has enough room, in a patch of ground called his territory, so that the couple can mate. A fourth purpose is to tell rival males to keep away.

As the partners come together, the male usually clasps the female from behind, in a tight grip. After a time she lays her eggs, and he sheds his sperm over them, to fertilize them and begin their development. In most cases, the adults then wander off, and leave the eggs and young. Only a few kinds of frog make caring parents!

▼ Chains of eggs
A pair of frogs or toads may stay clasped together for hours, even days. They usually lie low and keep quiet, to avoid catching the attention of predators. This pair of common toads is mating in a garden pond. The female is laying her chains of eggs onto the water weed.

▼ A slippery grip
Sometimes several male frogs all struggle to grab hold of the same female. The strongest one wins the tussle and gets to fertilize the eggs, an example of "survival of the fittest". These marsh frogs, also known as laughing frogs, are in a puddle in Portugal, Europe.

BEWARE: FROGS AND TOADS CROSSING!

Sometimes roads are built near ponds and marshes which frogs and toads have used for many years. As they migrate back each spring, they have to cross the road, and many are killed by traffic. In some places signs are put up in the spring, warning drivers to take extra care.

GROWING UP

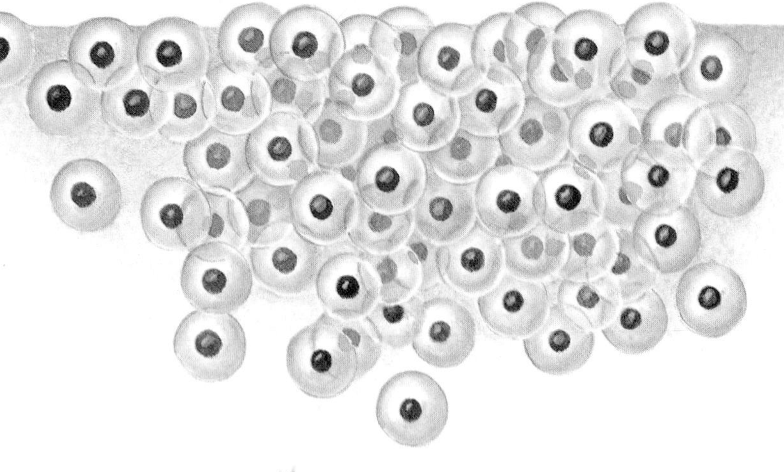

A frog begins life as a tiny black dot in the middle of its jelly egg. Soon it develops a head and tail, and wriggles out of the jelly to become a swimming tadpole. Then one of nature's most amazing changes takes place. The tadpole gets bigger, it grows legs and arms, and it loses its tail. At last it is a miniature adult – a froglet or perhaps a toadlet.

Few animals alter their body shape so much during their life as the frog. It changes from a round egg when it is laid to a tadpole with a tail and no limbs, and then to an adult with limbs and no tail! This process is called metamorphosis, which means "changing shape".

Most frogs and toads lay their eggs in water. The tadpoles hatch after a couple of weeks, depending on the temperature. They stay in the water for a few more weeks, swimming about as they feed on

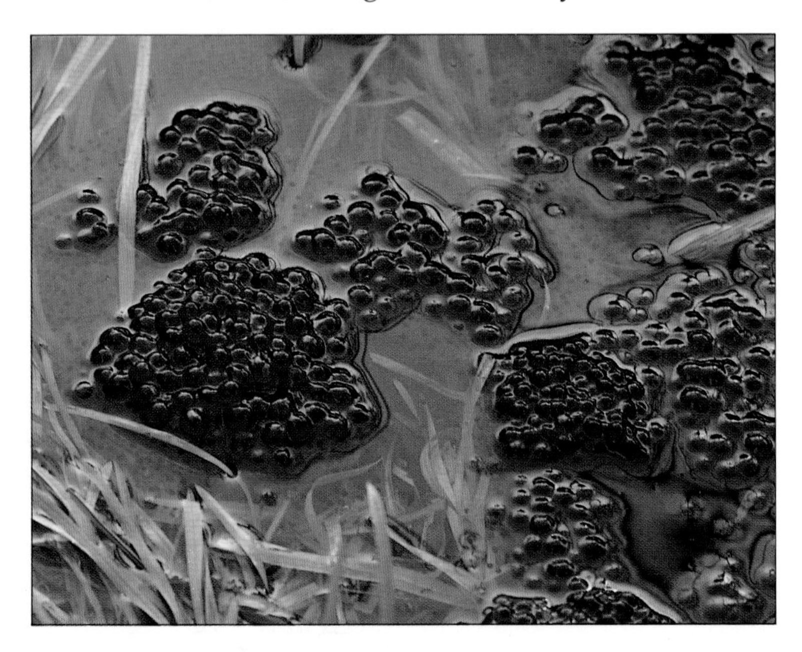

▲ Frog spawn
Each black dot, at the centre of the egg, is a developing tadpole. At this early stage it feeds on yolk, a nourishing substance which makes up part of the egg. Frog spawn usually floats in clumps, like this. A common European frog lays 1,000 to 3,000 eggs each year.

◄ Toad spawn
The common European toad lays its eggs in a long "necklace", wrapped around rocks and the stems of water plants. The eggs are in two strands inside, and the whole necklace may be 3 m (10 ft) long. Like the common frog, each female toad produces around 1,000 to 3,000 eggs.

◄ Protected in jelly
When a frog or toad lays her eggs, the jelly around each one is very thin. It swells quickly as it absorbs water to form a slimy, slippery mass. The jelly protects the eggs from the cold and from predators. It also absorbs heat from the sun and keeps the eggs slightly warm, so that they develop faster.

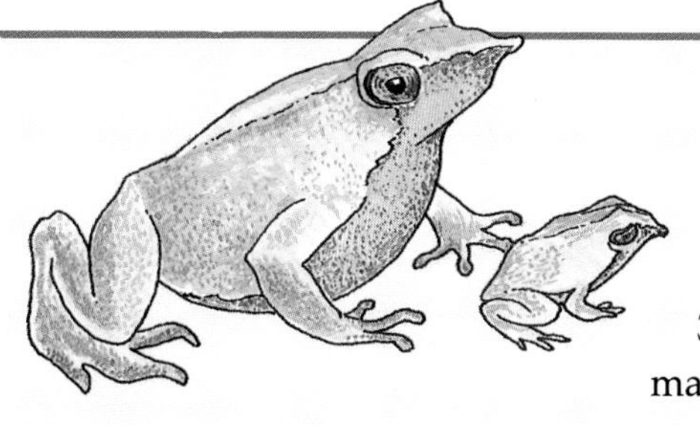

A MOUTHFUL OF BABIES

The 3 cm (1 in) long Darwin's frog live in cool forest streams in southern South America. It is named after its discoverer, the famous naturalist Charles Darwin. The female lays about 30 eggs, and the male guards these for around two weeks. Then he picks up about 15 of them and keeps them in his mouth! The tadpoles develop in his baggy chin skin, feeding on their egg yolk. When they are tiny froglets, only 1 cm (½ in) long, they swim away in the water.

PIGGYBACK EGGS

As she mates, the Surinam toad from South America collects her 50 or so eggs on the soft, sticky skin on her back. The skin folds over them and the tadpoles develop inside these tiny pockets on her back. They emerge three months later as little toadlets.

▼ This Surinam toad has just mated. The eggs stick to her back, ready to be covered by the skin fold.

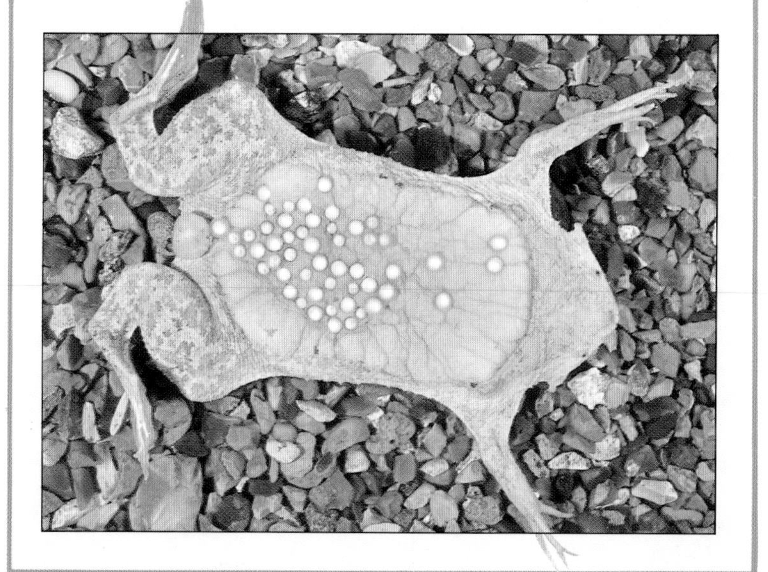

▲ The male midwife
A midwife is the name given to a woman who helps at the birth of a human baby. The midwife toad does the same job, except that "she" is a male. After the midwife toad's partner has laid a string of 50 eggs, he twists them around his legs and carries them everywhere he goes. If they dry out, he dips them in a puddle or stream to keep them damp. Four to five weeks later, he puts them in a pool, and the tadpoles hatch and swim off. Midwife toads live in woods and meadows in western Europe.

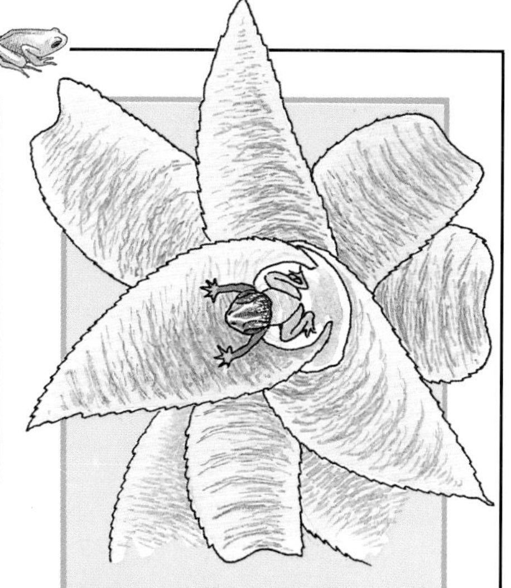

MINIATURE POND

Fingernail-sized bromeliad frogs mate and lay their eggs high above the ground, in the rainforest. They use a tiny puddle of water that has collected in a container formed by the leaves and petals of the bromeliad flower, a beautiful bloom which grows high up in the fork of a tall tree.

water plants. They breathe through their feathery gills which stick out on either side of the tadpole's head and absorb oxygen from the water.

As a tadpole grows, great changes happen inside as well as outside its body. The feathery gills shrink and the lungs grow in the body. The tadpole starts to take gulped breaths of air. It eats fewer leaves and other plant parts, and it begins to feed more on tiny water creatures and other bits of meat.

Getting ready to leave the water

The changes in the tadpole's body are controlled by hormones, body chemicals which make certain parts shrink as others develop. Gradually the

▼ From eggs to froglets
The eggs of a common frog develop among waterweeds and reed stems. Often the batches of eggs from several females clump together in a great floating mass.

▼ Hatching
About two weeks after being laid, the first tadpoles wriggle out of their jelly. They are shaped like commas and they may eat some of the jelly as their first meal.

▼ Back legs first
The young tadpoles feed by scraping the thin green growths off waterweeds. By four weeks their feathery gills have gone. Three weeks later, the back legs pop out.

▲ Green eggs
A glass frog has laid its small clump of eggs on this glossy leaf, in a tropical forest in northern South America. The greeny yolk helps to camouflage the eggs against the leafy background. The tadpoles will struggle free – and drop to the ground. But this should be safe, since the parent lays the eggs on a leaf overhanging a small creek or pool.

tadpole gets its limbs. Usually the legs come first, then the arms. Its tail shrinks as it is absorbed into the body. And finally the tadpole is a tiny froglet, breathing air and hunting prey, just like its parents. Within a few years it will grow as big as them.

This is the story of a typical tadpole, from a frog or toad. But there are many, many variations. Some parent frogs lay their eggs on land, in a damp place where the eggs do not dry out. The tadpoles grow quickly inside their jelly coat, feeding on nourishing yolk in the egg, and hatch as fully-formed froglets.

Tadpoles under the skin

Some frog and toad parents look after their eggs and young, especially those frogs and toads that live mainly on land. They carry the eggs wrapped around their legs, or protect them in "pockets" in the skin of their backs, or even inside their mouths or stomachs! The baby frogs wriggle out and hop free when they have developed.

Some tadpoles grow into adults in a few days. These are usually desert-dwellers. The parents quickly get ready to breed at the first sign of rain, and lay the eggs, within days, in pools and puddles. It then becomes a race, typical of many in nature, between the tadpoles hatching and growing up, and the puddles drying out under the hot desert sun.

▼ Front legs last
Gradually the tadpoles eat more meat, such as small water creatures. The front legs form some 12 weeks after hatching.

▼ Shrinking tail
The last main change, on the outside, is when the tail shrinks away. The froglet now breathes air and comes to the surface often.

▼ Leaving the water
Of the thousands of eggs, only a few dozen have grown into baby frogs. The rest were eaten by fish, diving beetles and other pond hunters.

HITCH-HIKING HATCHLINGS

A dozen or so tadpoles lie quietly on the back of their father, a Colostethus frog from rainforests on the tropical island of Trinidad, West Indies. In the breeding season, he turns much darker in colour, and guards the eggs where the female lays them. The tadpoles hatch and wriggle onto his back, where they stay for a few days. Eventually he takes them to water, so they can continue their development.

▲ The tadpoles, like their father, are in no danger of drying out in the damp, drippy mist of the rainforest.

LIVING IN A BACKPACK

Marsupial frogs carry their eggs in pouches or grooves in the skin on their backs. In the pygmy marsupial frog, from Venezuela in South America, the male fertilizes each egg as it is laid. Then he pushes it into the pouch on his partner's back.

▲ The pygmy marsupial frog has a clutch of about 10 eggs.

▼ When the tadpoles grow back legs, she lets them go.

LIFE IN WATER

It is much easier to move through air than water. Frogs that spend a lot of time in water have bodies that are specially suited to moving, breathing and eating there. Their long back legs, ideal for leaping on land, become strong kicking flippers, and their streamlined noses cut through the water. Did you know that, for its size, a frog swims over ten times faster than the speediest human swimmer?

Kept under water for too long, most frogs and toads would drown. Under the water, an inactive frog can take in enough of the oxygen dissolved in the water, through its skin, to stay alive. But a busy frog under the water needs more oxygen, to keep its muscles working. So it has to breathe air. Like you, it needs to reach the surface now and again, and take in lungfuls of fresh air.

The other great challenge of living in water is how to swim fast, to escape hunters and chase victims. Frogs which stay mainly in water have streamlined noses and bodies that cut down the resistance of the water. Their huge back feet splay open as they kick, to give a wide surface that pushes them along. A fast-swimming frog usually holds its front legs out of the way, against the underside of its body, for even better streamlining in the stream.

BREATHING UNDER WATER

Most frogs get only one-quarter of their oxygen through their skin. Yet a few frogs can live all their lives under water, never surfacing for a breath of air. They get all their oxygen through their skin. To make the most of the dissolved oxygen in the water around them, they have extra flaps or bits of skin. These give a bigger surface for absorbing the oxygen.

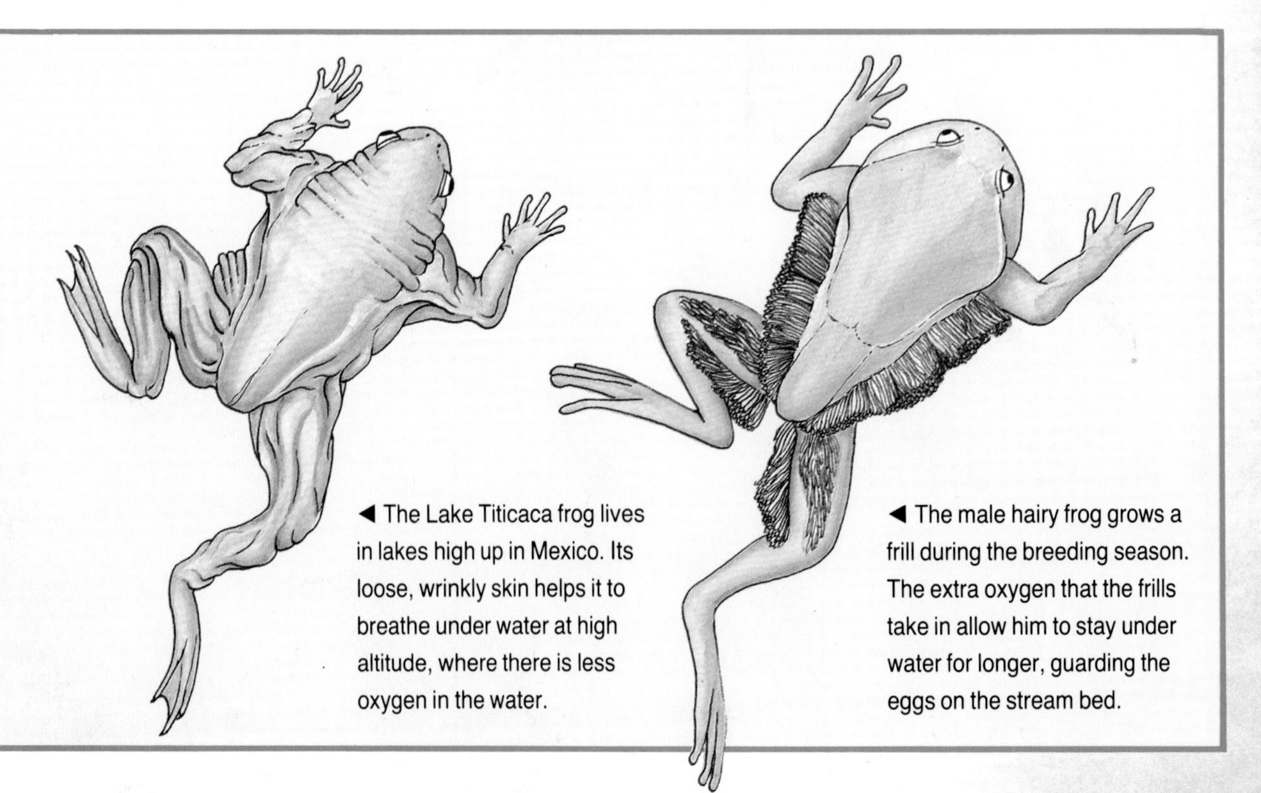

◀ The Lake Titicaca frog lives in lakes high up in Mexico. Its loose, wrinkly skin helps it to breathe under water at high altitude, where there is less oxygen in the water.

◀ The male hairy frog grows a frill during the breeding season. The extra oxygen that the frills take in allow him to stay under water for longer, guarding the eggs on the stream bed.

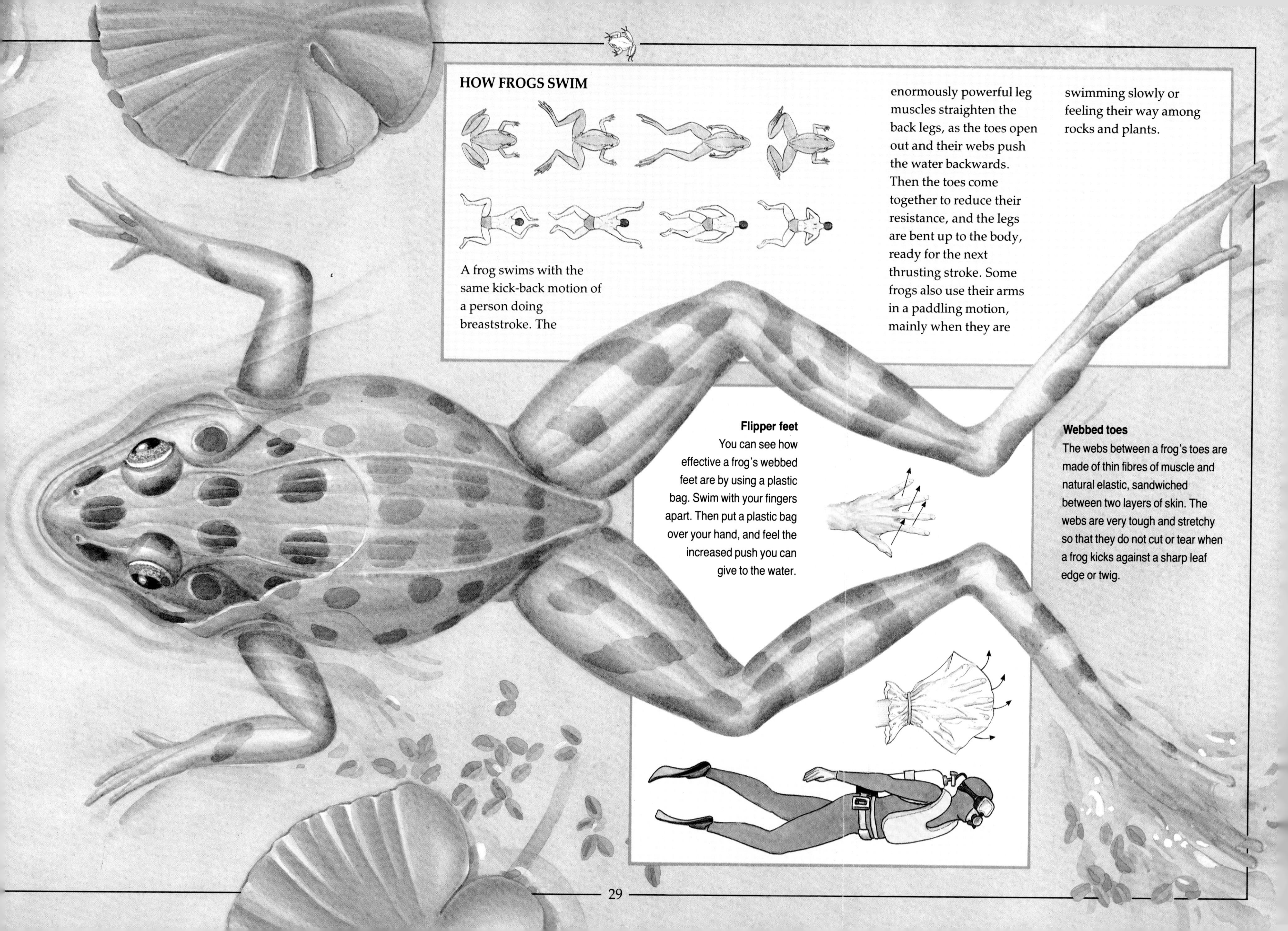

HOW FROGS SWIM

A frog swims with the same kick-back motion of a person doing breaststroke. The enormously powerful leg muscles straighten the back legs, as the toes open out and their webs push the water backwards. Then the toes come together to reduce their resistance, and the legs are bent up to the body, ready for the next thrusting stroke. Some frogs also use their arms in a paddling motion, mainly when they are swimming slowly or feeling their way among rocks and plants.

Flipper feet
You can see how effective a frog's webbed feet are by using a plastic bag. Swim with your fingers apart. Then put a plastic bag over your hand, and feel the increased push you can give to the water.

Webbed toes
The webs between a frog's toes are made of thin fibres of muscle and natural elastic, sandwiched between two layers of skin. The webs are very tough and stretchy so that they do not cut or tear when a frog kicks against a sharp leaf edge or twig.

A FROG'S DAY

Frogs and toads live all kinds of lifestyles. Some are active in the daytime, others at night. Some spend their time lying in wait for prey, or lying still to avoid predators, or simply lying. Others, especially small frogs in tropical forests, are always hopping and jumping about.

A frog's life is ruled by the temperature of its surroundings. This is because frogs are cold-blooded. They cannot make heat inside their bodies as we do. Internal warmth lets us stay active even in cold conditions. If a frog gets cool, its body works more slowly and it moves less and less. When a frog gets really cold, it hardly moves at all.

In most tropical forests, it's warm both day and night, and all year round, too. Frogs are active most of the time. If there is a dry season, they may stay in a dark, moist place. Otherwise, their bodies are usually warm enough to move about and catch prey.

In lands like Europe and North America, with winter and summer seasons, frogs and toads use their behaviour to keep warm for as much of the time as they can. They may sit in the sun and soak up its heat, then they move into the shade before they become too hot and dry. In this way they are usually ready for rapid action, whether catching a fly or leaping to safety from a snake.

▼ Dawn
The leopard frog lives in places across North America. As the sun rises after the cool night, it basks in a marsh or pond to warm up.

▼ Midday
The glaring midday sun is too hot for the leopard frog so it hides under a shady stone. It may catch a small insect or spider that wanders past, but usually it has a quiet day.

SUNBATHE, THEN A COOL DIP

Unlike the leopard frog below, the green-and-gold bell frog, from south-east Australia, is active in the daytime. It is famous for sunbathing. This keeps its body very warm and ready for super-fast action. But the bell frog rarely strays far from water, such as a bulrush-fringed marsh. Then it can wet its skin easily with a quick dip.

▲ The sunbathing bell frog likes to keep its feet wet.

◀ A moist, mossy "sunbed" makes the air around the bell frog damp, even in the hot midday sun.

▼ Dusk
As the sun sets, the leopard frog comes out to catch the last rays of warmth. Then it sets off on its nightly hunting trip.

▼ Midnight
Worms, moths, spiders, woodlice, and small water creatures are all in danger from disappearing into the leopard frog's wide mouth. As the night continues, the frog becomes cooler, and takes a rest . . . until the sun comes up again.

FROG FOOD

All frogs and toads are killers, and they eat their victims alive. They grab, gulp and crush their prey, swallowing it whole. A few frogs are fussy and snap up only one kind of food, such as termites. Others eat any living creature that they can stuff into their wide, gaping mouths.

▶ Favourite meals
Small animals without backbones, known as invertebrates, like insects, spiders and worms, form the mainstay of a frog or toad's diet. The bigger the frog, the bigger the prey it can tackle. Huge frogs like the bullfrogs and marine toads can eat mice, small rats, baby birds, lizards and snakes. In the water, big frogs devour fish, pond worms, water snails and even small crabs.

▼ Stage 1: The approach
In the half-light of evening, in the damp grass at the edge of a meadow, this small grasshopper is busy chirping to other grasshoppers. It hasn't noticed that the common toad, attracted by the noise, is creeping up slowly behind. For a time, the grasshopper sits still and listens to the singing of its neighbours. The toad seems to lose interest, and is almost ready to move on when the grasshopper's legs move rapidly as it chirps again . . .

▼ Stage 2: Take aim
. . . The toad is attracted again by the grasshopper's movements. It shifts its head to the side slightly, to judge the distance more accurately. Then it tenses its mouth and tongue muscles . . .

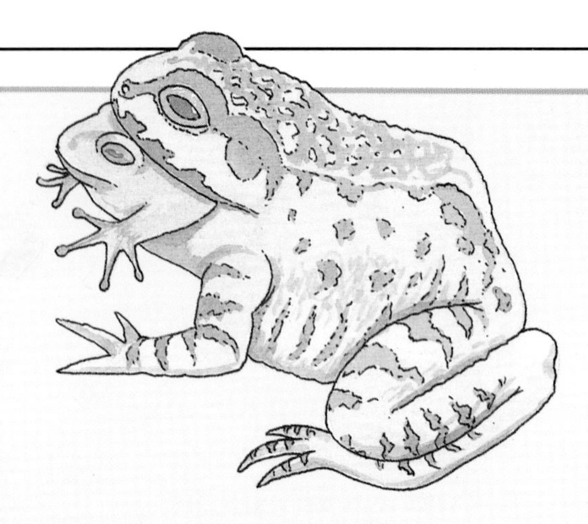

CARNIVORE, AND CANNIBAL

Frogs and toads are called carnivores, because they eat the flesh of other animals. (Creatures that eat plants are known as herbivores.) Most animals do not eat members of their own kind, but frogs and toads do. Big frogs may eat smaller ones of other species or even of their own kind. Eating members of your own species is called cannibalism, and it is most common in frogs and toads when other food is scarce. The big, strong bullfrogs are well-known small-frog eaters. Some frogs even chomp up their own tadpoles which hatched from the eggs they laid. Fancy eating your own children!

▼ Gotcha!
If a frog judges its prey to be too far for its tongue, it may leap up and grab it in its mouth in mid-air. In an instant, this common frog works out the hoverfly's speed and direction of flight, launches itself into the air, and catches its snack in mid-flight.

▼ Stage 3: The tongue-flick
The toad's long tongue shoots out and traps the grasshopper on its slimy, sticky tip. Before it can give a protest kick, the unfortunate victim is whisked back into the toad's mouth. The whole process is so quick that a person watching would just see the grasshopper disappear, as though by magic. The only clue may be a wing or feeler poking out of the toad's mouth.

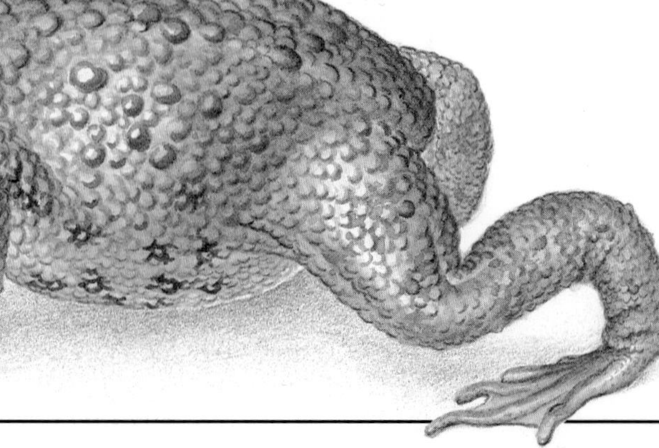

▼ Spiders
Spiders are hunters themselves, with a strong bite and poisonous fangs. Yet whether large or small, they make a tasty meal for a frog.

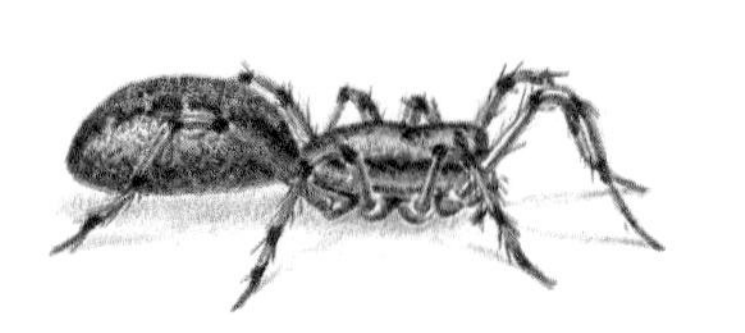

▲ Worms
All types of worms, from tiny roundworms like threads of cotton to huge juicy earthworms, help fill a gap in the frog's empty stomach.

◀ Flying insects
The hoverfly is a stingless fly that looks rather like a wasp. But toads eat them, as well as bees. They are not much bothered by the stings.

▲ Running insects
Ants squirt stinging formic acid at their attackers, but frogs and toads snap them up just the same.

▲ Slugs and snails
Slimy but nourishing, slugs are the enemy of the vegetable gardener. The hungry frog or toad is the gardener's friend. A few of the larger frogs can even crush snail shells.

Frogs hunt mainly by sight. Their large, bulging eyes probably have a different view of the world from ours, and they may not be able to make out so many colours or small details. But what a frog does see very clearly is any small movement. Special "bug detectors" in its eyes observe the slightest motion, down to the twitch of a gnat's leg.

The frog's two eyes, set on either side of the head, each see a slightly different view of the scene. The frog judges distance by this, and strikes as the victim comes near. But it only stays interested if the prey keeps moving. A creature which keeps still for a few minutes is safe, as the frog wanders off.

Mouths and tongues

The typical frog's hunting weapon is its tongue. This is fixed to the lower front of its mouth, and has a sticky tip. As the prey comes within reach, the frog flicks out its tongue, traps the prey on the end, and whips it back into its mouth. Big frogs and toads can reach prey that is further than 8 cm (3 in) away with their tongues.

Some frogs and toads have very small tongues, like the green-and-gold bell frog on page 31. They trap their food by lunging forwards and biting at it. Sometimes they use their hands to pin it down or cram it into the mouth. A few water-living frogs and toads, like the Surinam toad, do not have a tongue. They grab their dinner with their fingers, and jerk their head forwards to swallow it.

▲ Wide-mouthed tree frog
This front view of Peters' grey tree frog, from East Africa, shows that a frog's mouth can be as wide as its whole head. Tree frogs are masters at catching fast-flying insects. Like a tiny computer, their brains can calculate where the insect will be at the split second their tongue or mouth makes contact. In the breeding season these grey tree frogs make foam nests on the branches of trees, where they lay their eggs.

CLAWS AND JAWS

The large, fierce South African clawed toad grows to more than 12 cm (5 in) in body length. It is one of the few species that lacks a tongue. It digs in the mud of lakes and ponds, and feels with its sharp-clawed hands for worms and water insects. It can chase fish and will eat tadpoles if they come too near.

DESERT FROGS

Deserts, with their sweltering sun and parched ground, may not look like a promising home for damp-loving frogs and toads. But when the rains come, the desert springs to life. In a few weeks, seeds grow and burst into flower. Insects hatch from their tough eggs. And frogs and toads leave their moist holes, deep underground, to mate and spawn in the ponds and puddles.

Some deserts are hot, others are cold, but they are all very dry. Even so, a few species of frogs and toads live there. Like other desert-dwellers, they

▼ The shy Spanish spadefoot
The Spanish spadefoot toad likes places with loose, sandy soil, where it is easy to dig down and hide by day. This shy individual is hiding its "spades", which are on the inner side of each back foot.

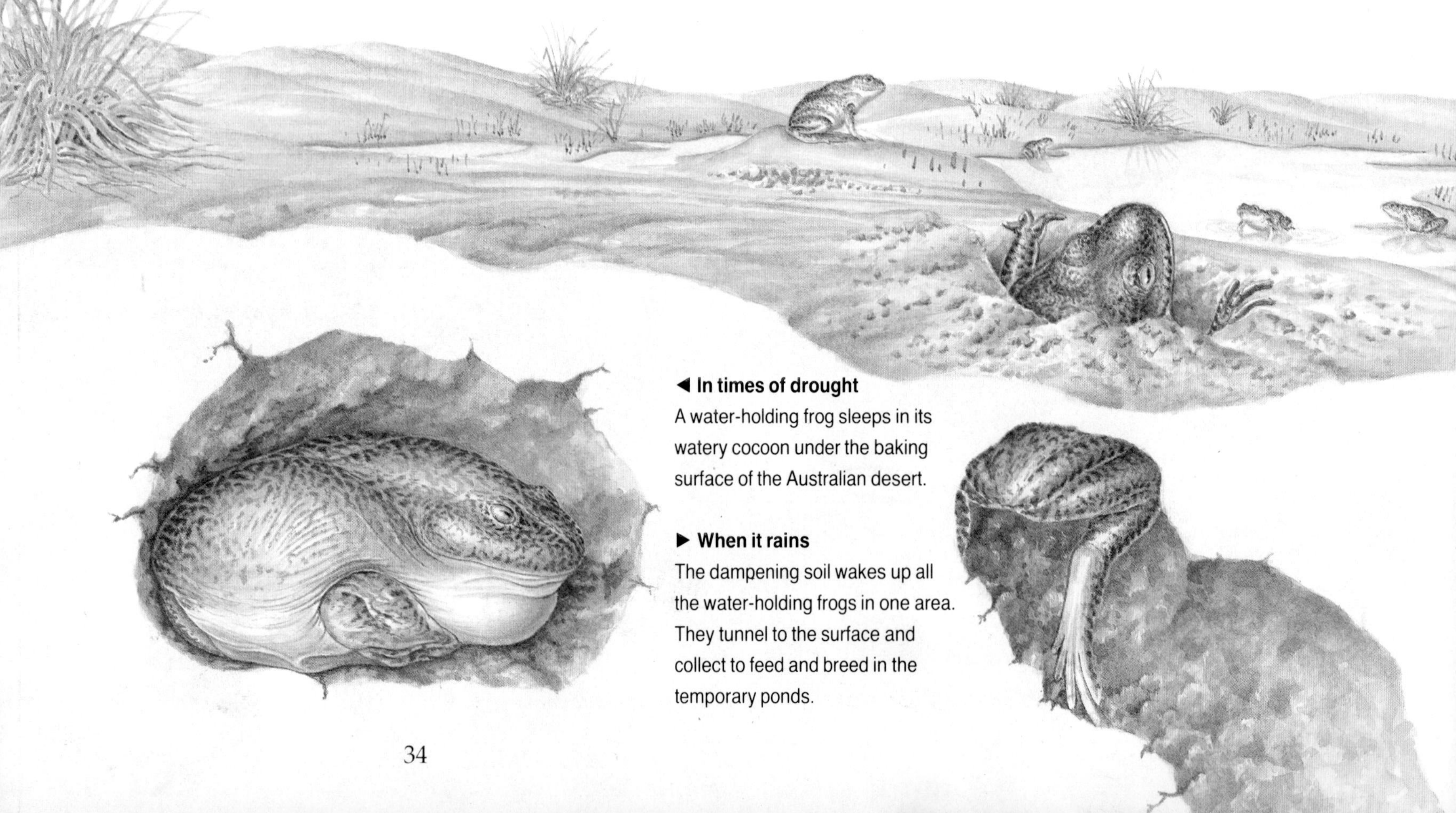

◄ In times of drought
A water-holding frog sleeps in its watery cocoon under the baking surface of the Australian desert.

► When it rains
The dampening soil wakes up all the water-holding frogs in one area. They tunnel to the surface and collect to feed and breed in the temporary ponds.

come out mainly at night, when the air is cool and the ground may be moist from dew. As day breaks, they burrow down and hide under the surface. Some toads have small, flat, hard lumps on their feet, like tiny spades, to help them dig. They are called spadefoot toads.

Underground, a frog or toad may eat the occasional worm or millipede that pokes into its burrow. But mainly it rests, away from the dryness and heat.

An underground pond

Desert frogs may not breed for years, if there is no rain. As soon as rains soak the ground, they come into breeding condition, mate and lay their eggs.

The water-holding frog does this, and it also has an amazing way of surviving the long droughts in the middle of Australia, where it lives. It digs a deep burrow, about 1m (3 ft) down, where water collects to form a private pond. It also stores water in its body, in its balloon-like, expanding bladder. It even sheds an unbroken outer layer of skin, and keeps a layer of water between this and its real skin. It can survive like this for months.

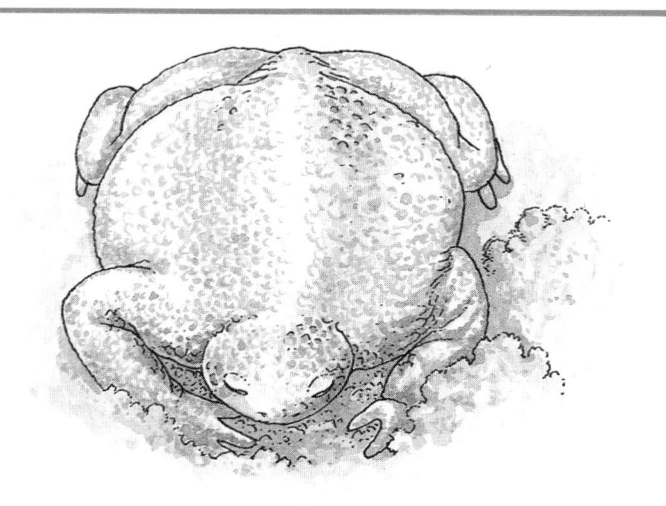

THE FROG THAT THINKS IT'S A MOLE

This Australian frog is sometimes called the turtle frog, thanks to its appearance, or the mole frog, because of its habits. It digs with its arms, head-first, unlike the spadefoot toads (below). It spends much of its life burrowing, like a mole, since it cannot walk very fast, and it can hardly swim at all.

DIGGING IN FOR A DRY SPELL

The plains spadefoot toad is found in drier areas of North America. As the photographs show, it is well camouflaged, and it can burrow backwards into the soil, to avoid predators or dryness. Their tadpoles eat the tadpoles of other frogs.

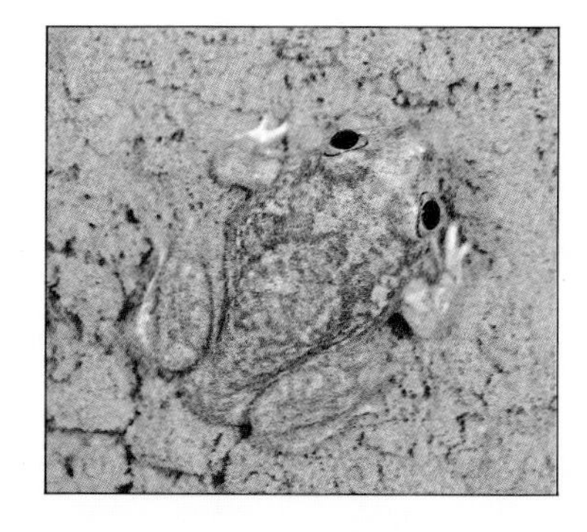

▲ **Going . . .**
The toad tests the soil to find a loose patch.

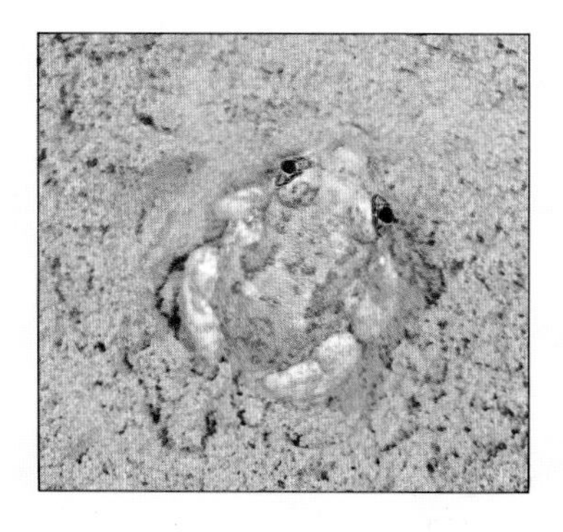

▲ **Going . . .**
It shuffles with its back feet and pushes the soil away.

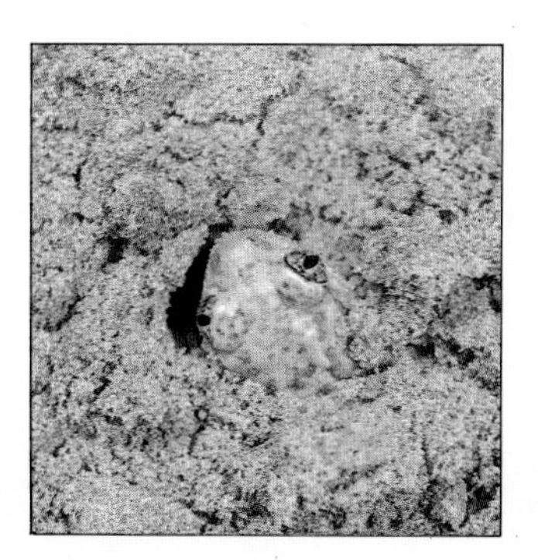

▲ **Gone (almost)**
In a few seconds, it has backed down into a safe hole.

Mountain Frogs

High up on the cold and windy mountain slopes, life is tough for any animal – and especially for frogs and toads. Few of them live at such high altitudes. Those that do have to cope with long freezing winters, drying summer winds, and air which has less oxygen than it does in the valleys far below. The frogs and toads that have conquered the mountains often struggle to make a living there.

Mountains are difficult places for any creatures to survive, even for mountain goats and mountain lions with their coats of thick hair. Frogs and toads find it especially hard. The wind, snow and ice make it tough for cold-blooded creatures. Insects and other suitable food are scarce, except during the brief summer.

The word "amphibian" comes from the Greek terms *amphi-* and *bios*, "both lives". It refers to their dual life, living mainly on land but breeding in water. On steep slopes, water rushes downwards. It rarely pauses to form quiet streams or pools. This lack of proper breeding sites is a major problem for mountain frogs and toads.

Like other animals that live at high altitudes, mountain frogs tend to be dark or black in colour. This is because a dark object soaks up more of the sun's warmth compared to a light-coloured one.

◀ Torrent frogs tend to stay at the stream's edge, out of the main current.

SIGNALS AT THE STREAMSIDE

This is one of the torrent frogs, which lives in fast-flowing streams up in the hills. This species comes from Borneo, in South-East Asia. Its large fingertips help it to cling to rocks in the fast-flowing water. Since its life is spent in gurgling, rushing water, any breeding calls would be drowned by the noise. So this little frog signals to others by raising its back foot, and spreading the toes to reveal the webs, which are bright blue!

A SINGLE MOUNTAIN FOR A HOME

Baw Baw frogs are found on one mountain only, in Australia – on Mount Baw Baw! They stay at heights above 1,500 m (5,000 ft), in the ice-cold rushing streams. They survive the coldest weather by hiding in thick bankside moss.

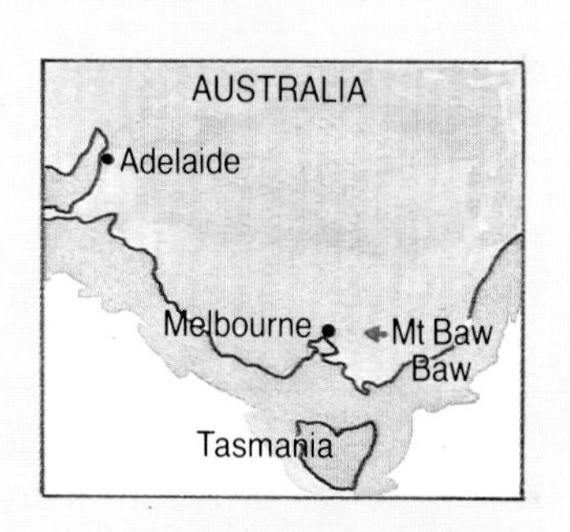

▲ Mount Baw Baw is part of the Great Dividing Range in south-east Australia.

▶ **Toad on the hill**
Boulenger's arrow-poison frog looks out over its home, the woody slopes of the Andes Mountains, in South America. Several members of its group, known as *Atelopus* toads, are mountain-dwellers in the region. Its bright yellow patches warn that it has poisonous skin.

NEW ZEALAND'S NATIVE FROGS

New Zealand has only three frog species of its own. Two of them are shown here. All the other frogs and toads on the islands have been introduced from other countries. The three original species can live in hills and mountains, and they are all very rare and protected by law. Their eggs are laid on land, in damp soil or under stones or logs. Each egg has a watery layer under its jelly, rather like a private pond. The tadpoles develop inside, hatching as froglets with almost-gone tails.

▲ Hochstetter's frog is found in several parts of New Zealand's North Island. It lays about 3 to 6 eggs only.

▲ Hamilton's frog survives only on a few islands in the Cook Strait, between North and South Islands.

FULL-TIME SWIMMERS

Frogs that rarely come out on land, even when they grow into adults, are not very common. Of the thousands of frog species, only a few dozens are known to live their entire lives in water. These full-time swimmers must be careful as they feed underwater, swallowing their prey of swishing fishes, wriggling worms, or thrashing water insects. If the frog gulps in a lungful or two of water, it could drown!

▶ Highly aquatic
The paradoxical frog dwells in ponds and lakes of the Amazon region, in the northern part of South America. It is also found on the nearby island of Trinidad. It is highly aquatic, which means it spends most – but perhaps not all – of its time in the water. It eats small fish, water worms and flies, and other insects that come near to the surface.

Long ago, in prehistoric times, amphibians were the first large animals to come out onto dry land. They did this partly to escape the big hunting fishes in the water. Also, insects, worms and other small creatures were invading the dry land, too. They were a new source of food, just waiting to be gobbled up. Since that time, relatively few frogs have stayed in the water or gone back to a full-time aquatic (water-dwelling) life.

Fully aquatic frogs include the African clawed toad, the Lake Titicaca frog (shown on page 28), and a strange toad from South-East Asia which has the scientific name *Pseudobufo subasper*, but no common English name.

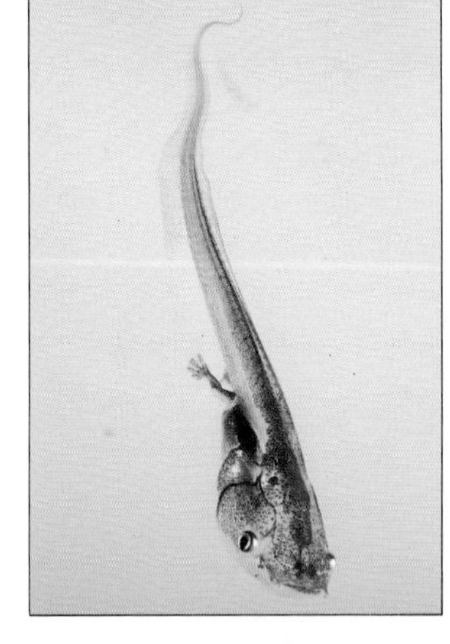

◀▼ Growing webbed feet
A tadpole of the South African clawed toad sprouts tiny back legs in the usual way (left), but as it grows into an adult (below), the legs and webbed feet grow even faster. Its nose and head are flattened and pointed, for underwater streamlining.
Another view of this toad is shown on page 33.

Sub-aqua breathing

Fully aquatic frogs absorb dissolved oxygen from the water around them, but most still come to the surface to breathe air into their lungs. Usually they take a quick "gulp" of air. Sometimes they lie at the surface and breathe like land frogs, by moving the flexible floor of their mouth and chin up and down, which pumps air into the lungs. Unlike ourselves, frogs cannot make their chests bigger to suck in air.

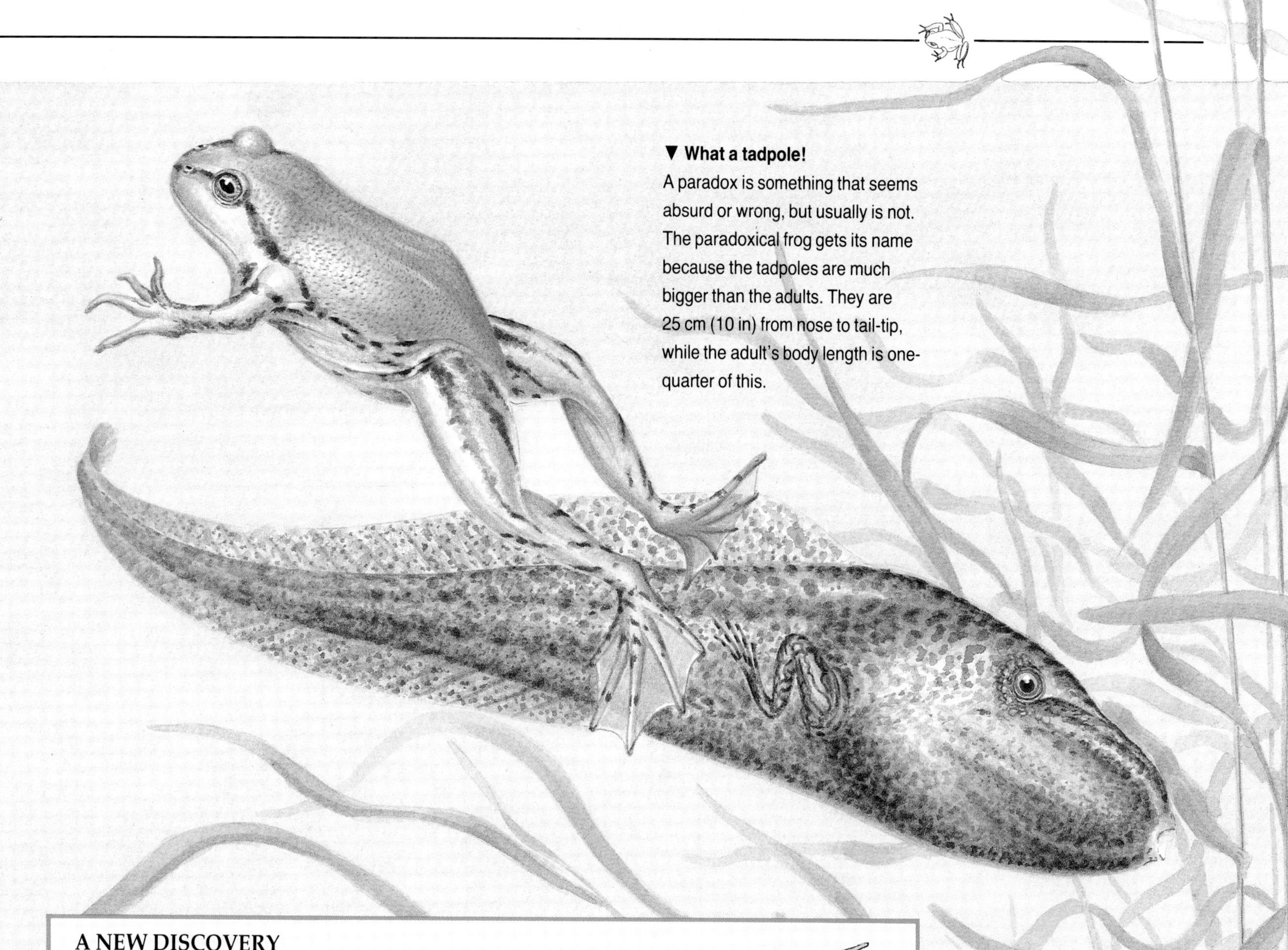

▼ What a tadpole!
A paradox is something that seems absurd or wrong, but usually is not. The paradoxical frog gets its name because the tadpoles are much bigger than the adults. They are 25 cm (10 in) from nose to tail-tip, while the adult's body length is one-quarter of this.

A NEW DISCOVERY

This 4 cm (1½ in) frog from Australia was only discovered in recent years. Its scientific name is *Rheobatrachus,* and its common English name is the Conondale gastric-brooding frog. It is thought to be the only Australian frog that lives almost entirely in water.

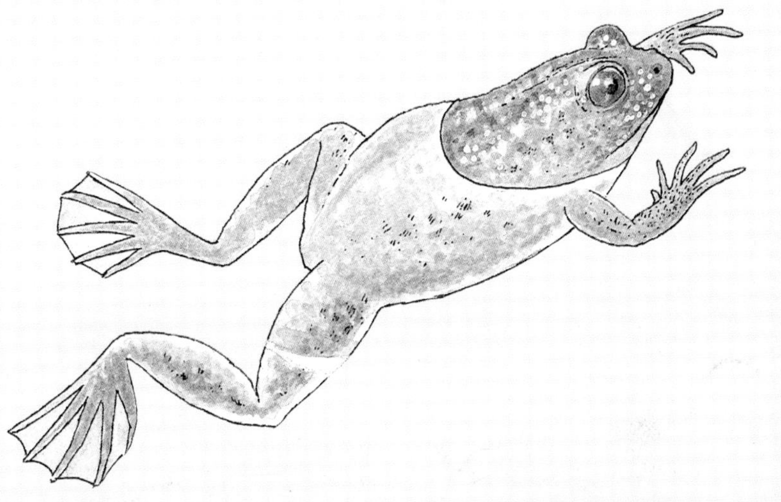

In Marshes and Swamps

Marshes, swamps, and boggy places are wonderful places for wildlife, especially frogs and toads. The pools and puddles are nurseries for the tadpoles, and there are plenty of drier patches for the adults to rest, with insects and worms to eat, and reeds and rushes to hide among. But swampy places are not much use to people – and here lies the problem. Many wetland areas have been filled in and cleared, for farmland, roads, and buildings; and so marsh and swamp frogs are now suffering as their world shrinks around them.

▼ The frog chorus
Chorus frogs are so named because they seem to sing together, like a choir, during the breeding season. They are small, light creatures and the reeds easily hold their weight, as they hold on with their long fingers and toes.

▶ The laughing frog
The marsh frog, 12 cm (5 in) long, is Europe's largest. It loves drainage ditches and dykes, and its croaks sound like human laughter.

A mosaic of pools, dampness and dry land is ideal for many kinds of frogs and toads. And this is what marshes and swamps offer. Some frogs crouch among the grasses and bulrushes around the edges of the water, while others swim out and mingle with the lilies and waterweeds. Even in colder regions, the depths of mud at the bottom of ponds and pools do not freeze in harsh weather. Frogs burrow down underground to spend the winter safe below the surface.

Fly food galore

Marshes are especially good for frogs because a host of insects lay their eggs in the pools. Among them are mayflies and caddisflies, damselflies and dragonflies, droneflies and midges, gnats and mosquitoes. The adult insects, and their young offspring developing in the water, are a rich source of food for toads and frogs.

DISAPPEARING FROGS

Land clearance affects many wild places where frogs and toads live. A further threat is capturing frogs to keep in captivity, as "pets" or for laboratory experiments. Rare frogs were once sold for large sums of money. In many countries, collecting is now illegal. Frogs and the places where they live are being protected by laws.

▲ Another threat is from pollution. Occasionally the damage is accidental, but often rubbish and chemicals are dumped into remote marshes in the hope that no-one will notice. The frogs do, and suffer as a result.

▼ Garden ponds are becoming important refuges for frogs and toads. A pond like this, fringed with rushes and reeds, makes a good replacement for a natural pool that has disappeared.

▲ A painted amphibian
The painted reed frog, from South Africa, looks as though someone has painted white stripes on its back. It belongs to a group of about 50 species, the hyperoliid frogs, that climb well. They live among sedges and reeds around fresh water. One new habitat they have found is on the edges of lakes and reservoirs behind dams.

▼ Sitting on a lily pad
Lily leaves float well and make ideal places for frogs to bask in the sun, and watch for prey. At the approach of danger, this common European frog slips away into the water.

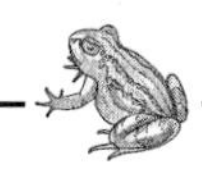

Frog Paradise

Tropical forests are the richest places in the world for wildlife, including amphibians. More than four-fifths of all frog and toad species come from the tropics and subtropics. They love the warmth and the dampness of the rainforests and the cloudforests on tropical hillsides. Some tropical places are so remote that there may well be new species of frogs waiting to be discovered.

On a journey from the ground up to the treetops of a damp tropical forest, you would meet a huge variety of frogs and toads – if you could find them! Many are small and very successfully camouflaged, others simply leap away before you can spot them.

On the forest floor, among the leaf-litter and rotting logs, hide brown frogs and toads that look just like the dead leaves around them. Another group of frogs climb among the vines, creepers, and lower branches of the trees, looking for flies and wood-eating insects. Higher still, bright green tree frogs with saucer-shaped toes clamber among the leaves, and bask in the sunshine way up above the ground.

▲ Leave us alone!
Green tree frogs pretend to be leaves and buds on a branch in the subtropical Everglades, in Florida, in the south-eastern United States.

◀ One in a million
The litter toad from Costa Rica, Central America, looks exactly like an old brown leaf – one of millions on the forest floor.

▼ Bullfrog
The African bullfrog can live in a range of different surroundings, from open grassland to forests. It is big and strong enough to eat mice, small birds, lizards, and even other frogs.

▼ Glass frog
The glass frogs of South America are so named because their skin, especially around the underside, is transparent. They cling to ferns and flowers with their sticky fingertips.

▲ A colourful harlequin
The bright colours of the harlequin frog, from the cloudforests of Central America, warn that it is poisonous.

► Ready for take-off
A Costa Rican flying frog prepares to leap from a leaf. It will glide down on the parachute-like webs of its hands and feet. (Another view of this frog is shown on page 11.)

► Red eyes at night
The red-eyed tree frog hunts at night, among the bushes and creepers of steamy Central American forests.

◄ Smaller than its name
Many tropical frogs are known only by their tongue-twisting scientific names. This thumb-tip sized frog is in the *Eleutherodactylus* group.

► Poison frog
This is one of the dozens of brightly coloured tropical frogs, called poison-arrow frogs, from Central and South America (see page 18). They live in groups near creeks and marshes.

FROG ENEMIES

A great array of hunting creatures enjoy snacking on frogs, or even toads. Because of the frog's dual life, both in and out of water, the frog runs into two sets of predators. On land these include birds, lizards, and snakes. In the water are sharp-toothed fish, mammals such as otters and water shrews, and wading birds – and those dreaded snakes again!

The lifestyle of the average frog keeps it out of the way of most creatures who would like to swallow it. Hiding under stones or leaves, and often well camouflaged, toads and frogs generally succeed in keeping a low profile. But, as if to make up for this safe and secure lifestyle, their list of predators is very long. It includes land and water birds, such as crows, blackbirds, and ducks. Herons in particular hunt frogs and toads through the reeds of the world's swamps and marshes. The heron stands completely still until the frog betrays itself by moving, then grabs or spears it with its long, sharp beak.

FROG ON A PLATE

Animals are not alone in liking to eat frogs. People like to eat them too. In many countries frogs are considered a great delicacy. The edible frogs of Europe have been cooked and eaten for centuries, and are especially popular in France. The flesh tastes rather like chicken. In fact, the scientific name for the edible frog is *Rana esculenta* which in the Latin language means "frog that is good to eat"!

Among mammal frog-eaters are rats and foxes, and hedgehogs and cats. Reptile enemies vary from lizards to the ever-threatening snakes. In tropical countries, there are also worm-like amphibians called caecilians (described on page 11) that prey on small frogs. Frogs are also victims of small creatures that cannot be seen without a microscope. These "parasites" exist inside or on the frog's body, taking away some of the frog's food before the frog has a chance to digest it completely.

Young frogs and toads, in the shape of tadpoles, are the most frequent victims of frog enemies. A common frog or toad produces thousands of tadpoles, yet usually only one or two survive – to become breeding adults two or three years later. The rest are eaten by sticklebacks and other small fish, diving beetles, dragonfly young, and by many other pond and stream hunters.

▲ **I'm poisonous!**
Have you learned by now, as predators have, what the bright colours mean on an arrow-poison frog?

▲ **Deadly enemy**
Snakes are seldom put off by the slimy or horrible-tasting skin of frogs and toads. This grass snake is about to try and swallow a common European toad.

▲ **Zig-zagging to safety**
If you surprise a frog, it may well leap away in a series of zig-zag jumps. These sudden changes in direction are designed to throw any pursuing predator off the trail. The frog heads for the nearest shadows or a clump of plants.

▶ **All's quiet at the pond**
It's a peaceful spring day, but can you spot the danger? Suddenly . . .

▶ **Leap to freedom**
. . . frog predators strike without warning. The heron snatches one unlucky victim, while the snake is ready to swallow another. The cat pounces on any stragglers.

THAT'S INCREDIBLE!

As creatures go, frogs are mostly small, slippery, and secretive. Yet there are many amazing facts and figures relating to them. For their size, they are one of the furthest jumpers and have some of the strongest poisons and strangest ways of rearing their young in the animal world.

▼ A harmless-looking toad
The fire-bellied toad sitting in a rice paddy field in eastern Asia, is unsurprisingly coloured green and black, but its name gives a clue to this toad's defence.

Herpetologists are scientists who study amphibians and reptiles. In the course of their work, they constantly discover more and more amazing facts about frogs.

In proportion to their body size, frogs are some of the greatest leapers in the animal kingdom. If a human, a kangaroo, and a frog were the same body size, there are no prizes for guessing who would outjump the others – the frog!

Very old toads

For their size, frogs and toads are amazingly long-lived. Some toads may survive over 40 years. Most mammals of the same size, such as rats or weasels, live for only a few years.

This is in contrast to the difficulty of surviving as a tadpole. In some small Asian frogs and toads, the adults lay their eggs in little pools of water that

► Long-jump champions
Imagine a human long-jumper, a kangaroo and an African sharp-nosed frog are all the same size – about 1.77 m (6 ft) tall (or long!)

◄ The human long-jumper
World-class human leapers can cover almost 9 m (30 ft) in a single bound. The kangaroo gets farther, as you can see on the right.

▼ A flaming red belly!
If the fire-bellied toad is disturbed, it faces the attacker and rears up to reveal its bright red-and-black underside! A pale whitish fluid oozes from its skin, which stings the mouth or eyes of the attacker. The fire-bellied toad is rather well named!

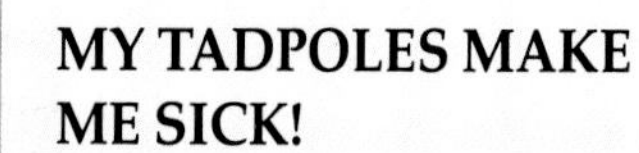

MY TADPOLES MAKE ME SICK!

The Australian Conondale frog (shown also on page 39) is a gastric brooder. It broods, or cares for, its eggs and tadpoles in its stomach. After her eggs are fertilized by a male, the female Conondale frog swallows them and keeps them in her stomach. She lies quietly in the water for several weeks as the tadpoles feed on their yolk in the eggs. The digestive chemicals that her stomach usually makes are not produced at this stage. Then she vomits up the froglets, just as if she were being sick, and they hop away!

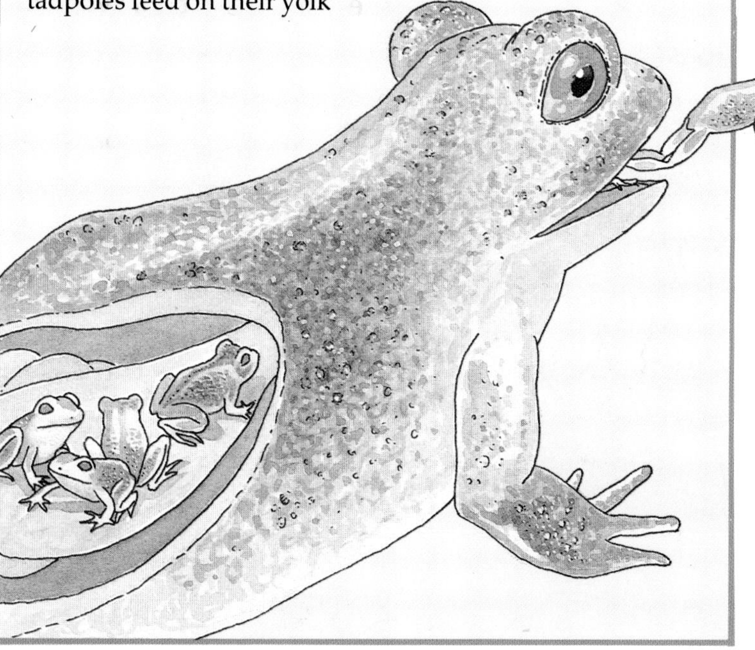

◀ The woolly jumper
A kangaroo's leap has been measured at about 13 m (43 ft). Compared to its body length, that's twice as far as a human. But for the African sharp-nosed frog, turn the page – twice!

collect among tree roots or in bamboo stems. The first tadpoles to hatch out eat the others. The mother has provided them with food – in the shape of their brothers and sisters.

Some frogs skip out the tadpole stage. The female lays a few large eggs with plenty of yolk, and the young then develop inside the egg capsules, hatching out eventually as fully-formed froglets, with arms and legs and no tail. In fact, as we continue to study frogs, especially in remote tropical areas, we find that this tadpole-less life style is not so rare as might be thought. More than 600 species may follow it – almost one-fifth of all frogs and toads!

Biggest, smallest and coldest

There are several claims for the biggest member of the frog-and-toad group. But what does "biggest" mean? In most frog species, females are bigger than males. The *longest* frog or toad is probably the goliath frog, a rare species from West Africa. (Length is measured in an official way, from the snout or front of the mouth to the vent, which is the rearmost part of the body.)

Likewise, there are many claims for the *heaviest* frog or toad. Some goliath frogs weigh over 3 kg (6½ lb). One huge American bullfrog was reported to weigh 3.2 kg (7 lb), but the heaviest official weight

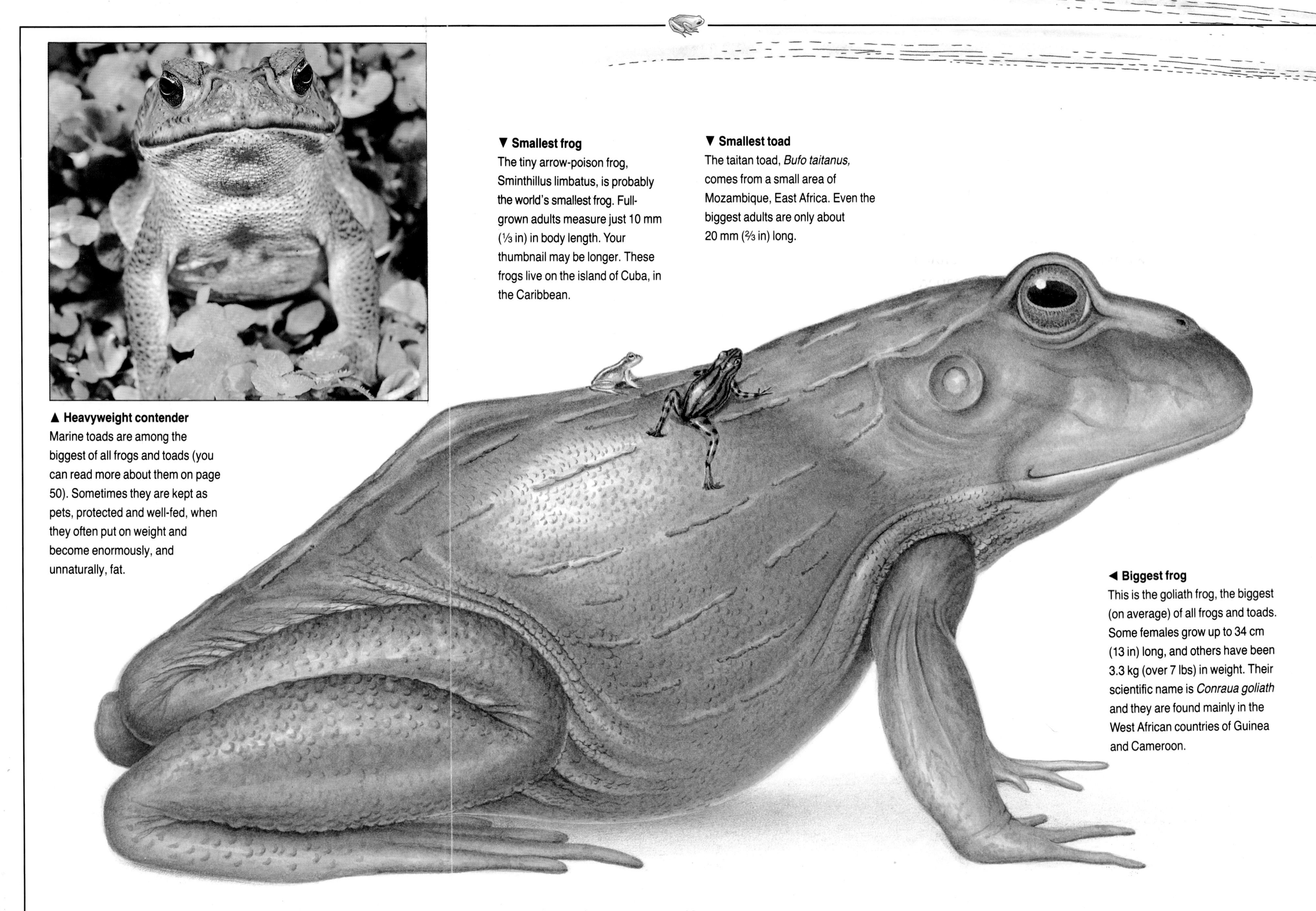

▲ Heavyweight contender
Marine toads are among the biggest of all frogs and toads (you can read more about them on page 50). Sometimes they are kept as pets, protected and well-fed, when they often put on weight and become enormously, and unnaturally, fat.

▼ Smallest frog
The tiny arrow-poison frog, Sminthillus limbatus, is probably the world's smallest frog. Full-grown adults measure just 10 mm (⅓ in) in body length. Your thumbnail may be longer. These frogs live on the island of Cuba, in the Caribbean.

▼ Smallest toad
The taitan toad, *Bufo taitanus,* comes from a small area of Mozambique, East Africa. Even the biggest adults are only about 20 mm (⅔ in) long.

◀ Biggest frog
This is the goliath frog, the biggest (on average) of all frogs and toads. Some females grow up to 34 cm (13 in) long, and others have been 3.3 kg (over 7 lbs) in weight. Their scientific name is *Conraua goliath* and they are found mainly in the West African countries of Guinea and Cameroon.

for this frog is around 600 g (21 oz). As a comparison, Europe's largest is the marsh frog, with a weight of slightly over 200 g (7 oz) and a length of 13 cm (5 in).

In the depths of winter, some frogs freeze almost solid, and then thaw out in spring! Spring peepers, grey tree frogs and striped chorus frogs are able to survive weeks spent with two-thirds of their bodies frozen as ice. Yet within hours of thawing out they go off catching flies.

FLYING FROGS

A few kinds of frogs can "fly" – or rather, glide. They spread their big webbed toes and parachute from a branch, swooping down onto another tree. They can cover 15 m (50 ft) in a single glide – it makes a useful escape route from enemies.

▶ Marsupial frogs
This is one of the marsupial frogs (see also page 27), whose tadpoles develop in a pouch or fold of skin on the mother's back. Marsupial frogs come mainly from South America. Some of the females carry more than 200 eggs on their backs, which are put there by the male after he has fertilized them. The eggs hatch and the tadpoles grow under the skin, over two or three months. The mother then splits open the pouch with her feet and tips the tadpoles into a convenient pool, where they finish growing to full-sized frogs.

▲ Running after a snail
The little natterjack toad of Europe has a clear yellow stripe down its back. Its legs are so short that it can hardly jump! Instead, it runs quite fast when it chases prey.

HELPFUL AND HARMFUL FROGS

Through the ages, frogs and toads have served humankind. They eat the slugs that damage vegetable crops and the flies that spread diseases. In a very few cases, frogs and toads have harmed people. But this is usually our fault – for trying to eat the poisonous kinds, or for bringing them to new places where they multiply out of control.

In general, frogs have been more helpful than harmful. They feed on many creatures which we think of as pests, like snails and mosquitoes. The tastier frogs are eaten in many regions, including one kind known as "mountain chicken" from the West Indies. Frogs have been used in the laboratory, where students cut them up to learn about biology, and they have also been used for finding out whether a woman was expecting a baby. The African clawed toad laid eggs when injected with the urine of a pregnant woman.

► A safe landing. After an enormous jump of 5 m (16½ ft), almost 100 times its body length, the African sharp-nosed frog (from page 46) lands on its shock-absorbing front legs. Our person-sized frog could have covered over 150 m (500 ft).

DANGEROUS IF TOUCHED

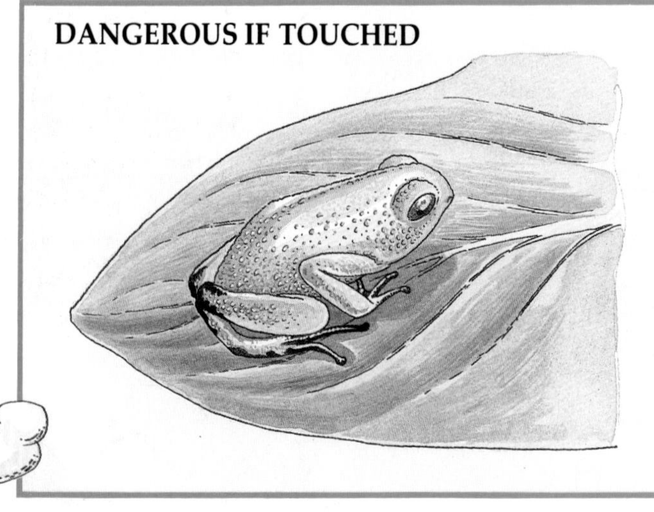

There are several kinds of arrow-poison frogs with venom strong enough to kill a human. The most poisonous is the bright yellow or gold *Phyllobates terribilis,* from Colombia in northern South America, which was discovered by scientists only in 1978.

FROGS AND TOADS IN MYTHS AND LEGENDS

Thousands of years ago, the Ancient Egyptians worshipped the god Heket, who had the body of a woman and the head of a frog. Since that time, frogs and toads have been popular in traditional tales and fairy stories all over the world.

▶ The poor toad has suffered from many untrue superstitions, such as the belief that touching it will give you warts. In 1908 Scottish writer Kenneth Grahame helped the toad's image when he published *The Wind in the Willows.* One of the book's stars was Toad of Toad Hall. Although boastful and deceitful, he had many lovable characteristics, particularly his energy and enthusiasm.

◀ Freak weather conditions sometimes bring strange rainshowers. Little froglets and toadlets are small enough to be picked up by strong winds, carried along in a cloud, and then rained down many miles away – still alive!

◀ The gardener's friend
Some gardeners dislike toads and frogs, but they are, in fact, useful creatures. They come out in the dampness of night and catch slugs and snails, which would otherwise gobble up the leafy vegetables, such as lettuces and cabbages.

THE CANE TOAD

The marine toad is often called the cane toad because it lives in the sugar-cane plantations of north-east Australia. It was taken there from South America in 1935, to help get rid of beetles and other sugar cane pests. Unfortunately, the toads took over and have become pests themselves.

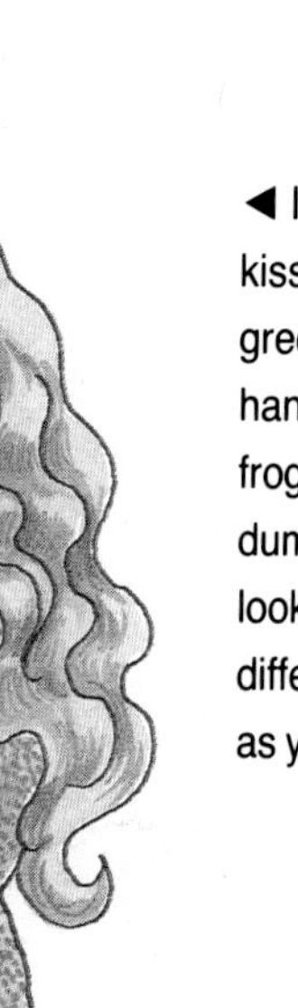

◀ In a number of fairy tales, a kiss from the princess turns a green, blinking frog into the handsome prince. The small frog, with its bulging eyes, dumpy body, and comical-looking grin, was about as different from the elegant prince as you could imagine!

▲ Toads, lovers of damp woodland night, were supposed to sit on seat-shaped fungi that were as poisonous as themselves. This may be where the name "toadstool" came from.

25 Essential Facts About Frogs

Even the world's greatest frog experts cannot know all the fascinating details about every frog and every toad – where they are found, what they look like, and how they live and feed and breed. This frog-packed fact-kit provides a handy summary of vital information about some of the most interesting, and misunderstood, creatures on Earth.

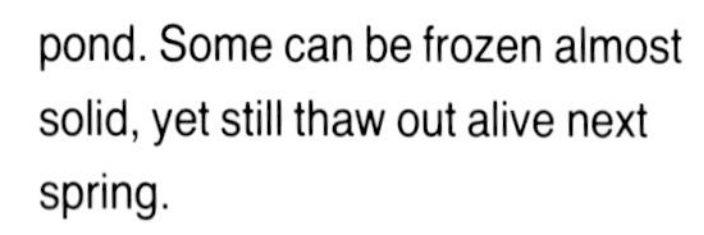

1 At home most places
There are almost 3,500 kinds, or species, of frogs and toads around the world. They live everywhere except the North and South poles, the seas, and the coldest mountaintops.

2 Two in one
Frogs and toads are amphibians. This word means "dual life", because most of them start their lives as tadpoles in water, then come out on land as they grow into adults.

3 No difference
Some people think of toads as fat, short-legged, and warty, while frogs are smooth, slim, and long-legged. But there is no real scientific difference between a frog and a toad. They all belong to the same group, *Anura,* which means "tail-less".

4 Tailed kin
Their closest relatives are newts and salamanders. These are also amphibians, but they have long tails.

5 Tropical types
Four-fifths of all frog and toad species live in the tropics and subtropics. They are mostly small and lively. New kinds are still being discovered in remote places.

6 Eat the lot
All frogs and toads hunt other creatures for food, such as beetles, slugs, worms, and flies. They usually swallow their victims whole and alive!

7 Ice in their veins
In regions with cold winters, frogs and toads burrow into the soil or into the mud at the bottom of a pond. Some can be frozen almost solid, yet still thaw out alive next spring.

8 Not only water
Some frogs live almost all their lives underground. Others live entirely in trees, or among dead leaves. Not as many as you think stay in water all the time.

9 Noises by boys
Frogs and toads croak and call mainly during the breeding season. The noisy ones are usually males, calling for a female partner or warning away rival males.

10 Named by noise
A frog's name may tell you about the sound of a frog's call, as in the spring peeper, bell frog, and barking frog.

11 Choosy parents
Some frogs breed only at a certain time each year, and lay less than 10 eggs. Others don't. The marine toad breeds whenever it can, and lays over 30,000 eggs each year!

12 Eggs in jelly
The typical female frog lays her eggs in water, ranging from a desert puddle to a fast stream or big lake. Frog eggs are covered in jelly and called spawn.

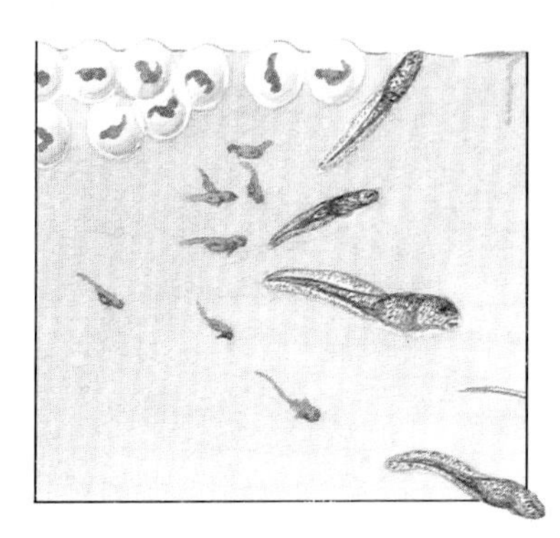

13 Frog young
They hatch into tadpoles, which have tails, and gills for breathing underwater.

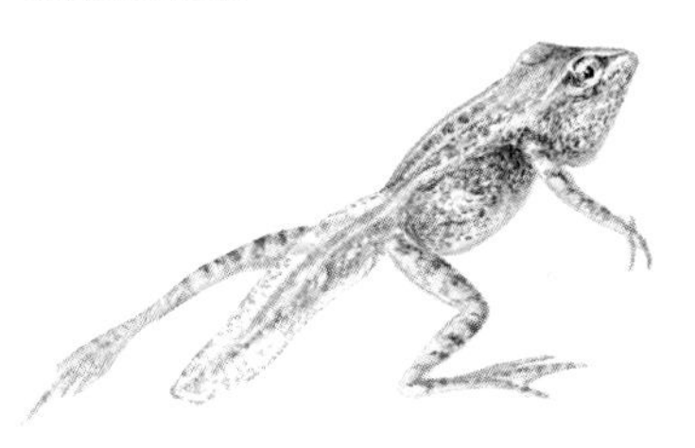

14 Sprouting and shrinking
As a tadpole grows up its gills shrivel, it develops lungs to breathe air, it sprouts four legs (back ones first), and its tail shrinks.

15 Meta-whatsits?
This amazing change in body shape, from the tadpole (which is known as a larva) to the grown-up adult frog, is called metamorphosis.

16 Developing everywhere
Some frogs look after their eggs and young. The tadpoles may develop on the parent's back, in its mouth, or even in its stomach!

17 Missing out
In damp tropical forests, hundreds of kinds of frogs have almost done away with the swimming tadpole stage. They lay eggs in damp places. The eggs develop inside their jelly coatings, and out hatch small but fully-formed froglets.

18 In through skin
A grown-up frog breathes oxygen from the air with its lungs. It also takes in some oxygen through its moist skin (on average, about one-quarter of the oxygen it needs).

19 Nasty taste!
Most frogs and toads have poison in their skin. This oozes out when they are attacked, making the enemy drop them and leave them alone afterwards. The arrow poison frogs from South America have specially strong poison in their skin. Some of these small, colourful frogs possess enough poison to kill several people.

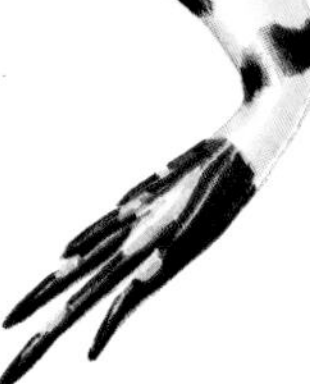

20 Dull and dazzling
Lots of frogs are coloured for camouflage. They are mottled greens and browns, to merge in with their background. Other frogs wear bright reds, oranges, yellows, and blues. These colours warn attackers of their poisonous skin.

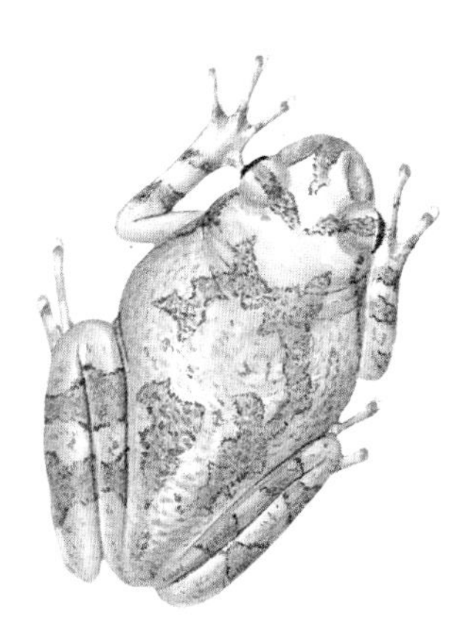

21 Little and large
The goliath frog is the biggest, over 34 cm (13 in) in body length. The tiny *Sminthillus* arrow poison frog is only 1 cm (½ in) long.

22 Look at them jump!
For their size, frogs are some of the greatest leapers in the animal world. The small African-sharp-nosed frog can cover 5 m (16 ft) in a single hop.

23 Our pals
In general, frogs and toads are helpful animals for humans. They eat flies, slugs, and other pests.

24 No room for frogs
More and more frogs are suffering from our activities. We fill in or pollute their breeding ponds, and take over the wild places where they live for farmland, roads, and buildings.

25 Save our frogs!
Some frogs and toads are on the official list of threatened animals. They need our help, before it is too late and they die out altogether.

GLOSSARY

(Note: Words in *italics* refer to other entries in the Glossary.)

Amphibian A member of the group *Amphibia* – a cold-blooded creature with a backbone and bony skeleton, that lays jelly-covered eggs which hatch into tadpoles. All frogs and toads, along with newts and salamanders, and *caecilians*, are amphibians. "Amphibian" means "both lives"; most amphibians begin their lives in water, but then live mainly on land when full-grown.

Amplexus When a male frog grips a female tightly at breeding time.

Anuran A member of the frog and toad group, which has the scientific name *Anura*, meaning "tail-less". All frogs and toads are anurans, and the *Anura* group contains only frogs and toads.

Aquatic Living mostly, or fully, in the water.

Bladder An expandable, balloon-like part inside the lower body, that stores wastes as urine.

Breeding The process of mating with a partner, and laying eggs or giving birth to young.

Bug detectors Special parts inside a frog's eye. They may not be able to see in great detail or distinguish lots of colours, but they are very sensitive to the tiniest movement.

Burrow To dig or tunnel into something and make a long hole in it, such as in the sandy soil of a desert, or in the bark of a tree.

Caecilian A type of amphibian with no legs, which looks more like a worm or snake. Caecilians live mostly in the soils of tropical forests.

Camouflage When an animal is coloured or patterned to blend in with its surroundings to avoid being detected.

Cannibal A creature that eats its own kind – it devours members of its own *species*.

Carnivore An animal that eats mainly the flesh and body parts of other animals. A herbivore, on the other hand, eats plants.

Cloaca The hole at the rear end of a frog's body, between its legs. Body wastes such as urine leave through it, as do the eggs in a female frog and the sperm in a male one.

Cocoon A bag- or sack-like structure, for enclosing and protecting something. A spider's egg cocoon contains its eggs, and many types of caterpillars spin themselves protective silk cocoons.

Cold-blooded Dependent on the temperature of the surroundings for body temperature. Unlike mammals and birds, cold-blooded animals are unable to make their own body warmth and stay active all the time. However this term is misleading since in the hot desert a "cold-blooded" frog may well be warmer than the "warm-blooded" desert fox that hunts it!

Courtship The process by which an animal selects and gets together with a partner for mating. Courtship may involve visual signs and displays, songs or calls or other sounds, and special smells, tastes, and touching.

Dyke A bank or barrier, often with a ditch or trench next to it. Dykes are made to keep out floodwater or to carry water to crops in the fields.

Evolution Change through time. All animal groups, from dinosaurs to frogs, have changed to become better suited to their surroundings, as the surroundings themselves change.

Feeler A long, thin body part, usually on the head, that is sensitive to touch, and often smells and tastes, too. In insects and similar creatures, the feeler is called an antenna.

Fertilize To join a sperm with an egg, and start them growing and developing together into a new living thing.

Froglet A common name for a young frog that has changed shape and is no longer a tadpole, but which is not yet full grown.

Fungi Living things that feed on the bodies of dying and dead animals and plants. Mushrooms, toadstools, and moulds are fungi.

Gastric brooder A creature that broods (cares for) its eggs and/or young in its stomach. A gastric-brooding frog swallows its eggs and the tadpoles develop inside its stomach.

Gills Special feathery or comb-like body parts, with a rich blood supply, designed for taking in oxygen dissolved in water. See also *Lungs*.

Gland A body part that produces a useful fluid or other substance, such as the lacrimal gland that makes tear fluid for the eyes. See also *Parotid gland*.

Gullet The tube down which food goes when it is swallowed, from the mouth to the stomach.

Habitat The type of place or countryside where an animal or plant usually lives. Tropical rainforest, coral reef, grassland, rocky seashore, and desert are all types of habitats.

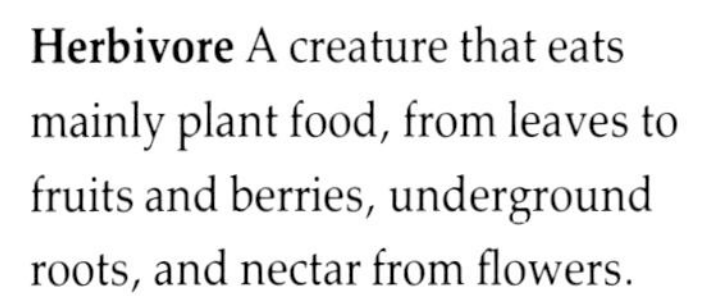

Herbivore A creature that eats mainly plant food, from leaves to fruits and berries, underground roots, and nectar from flowers.

Hormones Special body chemicals in a creature that control aspects of its growth, maturity, and behaviour. The change in shape from tadpole to frog is under the influence of hormones.

Invertebrate An animal without a backbone, such as an insect, spider, or worm. See also *Vertebrate.*

Larva The young or immature form of a creature that hatches from an egg. A larva does not look much like its parent. For example, butterflies have larvae called caterpillars, and frog larvae are known as *tadpoles.*

Lungs Special sponge-like or honeycombed body parts, with a rich blood supply, designed for taking in oxygen from the air. See also *Gills.*

Marsupial An animal with a "pocket" or "pouch" on its body, which is generally for protecting and raising its young. The official animal group *Marsupalia* includes kangaroos, wallabies, koalas, and possums.

Mating When a female and a male animal of the same kind come together, and the male's sperm fertilizes the female's eggs, so these can develop into babies.

Metamorphosis Drastic change in body shape, as when a caterpillar changes into a chrysalis and then a butterfly, or when a tadpole grows and changes into an adult frog.

Mimic In nature, an animal that looks or behaves like another, which is known as the model. Usually the model is poisonous or dangerous in some way. The mimic then gains protection, even though it may be harmless.

Mucus A slippery, slimy substance that coats the skin of many types of frogs and toads, as well as other creatures such as slugs and worms. It helps to prevent the body drying out, and makes it slippery and difficult for predators to grasp.

Paradox Something which sounds stupid or unbelievable or absurd, but which is (or might be) true.

Parotid gland A body part behind the ear or near the jaw. In frogs and toads it makes foul-tasting or poisonous fluid for protection against enemies. (In humans the parotid gland makes saliva, and it swells up painfully in the illness called mumps.)

Predator Any animal that hunts another for food.

Polar Near the Earth's North or South Pole, where the summer is short and the winter is long and bitterly cold.

Pollywog See *tadpole.*

Sac Any loose, expandable, balloon-like part, such as the *vocal sac* of a frog or toad.

Spawn The jelly-covered eggs laid by a female creature such as a frog, toad, or newt. Or the non-jelly-covered eggs released into the water by an animal such as a fish or starfish.

Species A single kind or type of animal. Members of a species look and behave much the same as each other, and they can breed together. But they cannot breed with a member of another species.

Subtropics The lands on either side of the *Tropics,* near the middle of the Earth, where it is warm for most of the year.

Tadpole A common name for the larva of a frog or toad (also known as a "pollywog").

Toadlet A common name for a young toad that has changed shape and is no longer a tadpole, but which is not yet full grown.

Tropics The lands on either side of the Equator, around the middle of the Earth, where it is warm for all or most of the year.

Tympanum Another name for the eardrum. In a human it is hidden inside the ear, but in a frog it is often clearly visible as a circle or disc of skin just behind the eye.

Vegetation A general name for the plants in a certain place, such as the bushes and trees in a wood, or the reeds and rushes around a pond.

Vertebrate An animal with a backbone – a spine or spinal column made of bones called vertebrate. The five main kinds of vertebrates are fish, amphibians, reptiles, birds, and mammals. See also *Inverbrate.*

Vocal cords Small ridges or strips of a tough body material, in the voice-box in the throat. They vibrate when air passes over them to produce sounds.

Vocal sacs Flexible balloon-like patches of skin, usually around the face or neck, that swell up with air as an animal makes its songs or calls. Many frogs and toads have vocal sacs, and so do animals like howler monkeys.

Warning coloration Bright colours and patterns which warn predators that the animal is horrible-tasting, or has a sting, or is poisonous or dangerous in some way.

Yolk The nourishing substance in an egg that a developing baby animal feeds on, before it is born or hatches and has to find its own food.

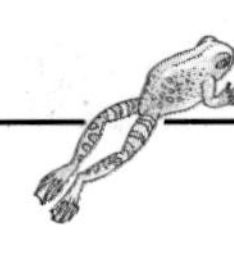

INDEX

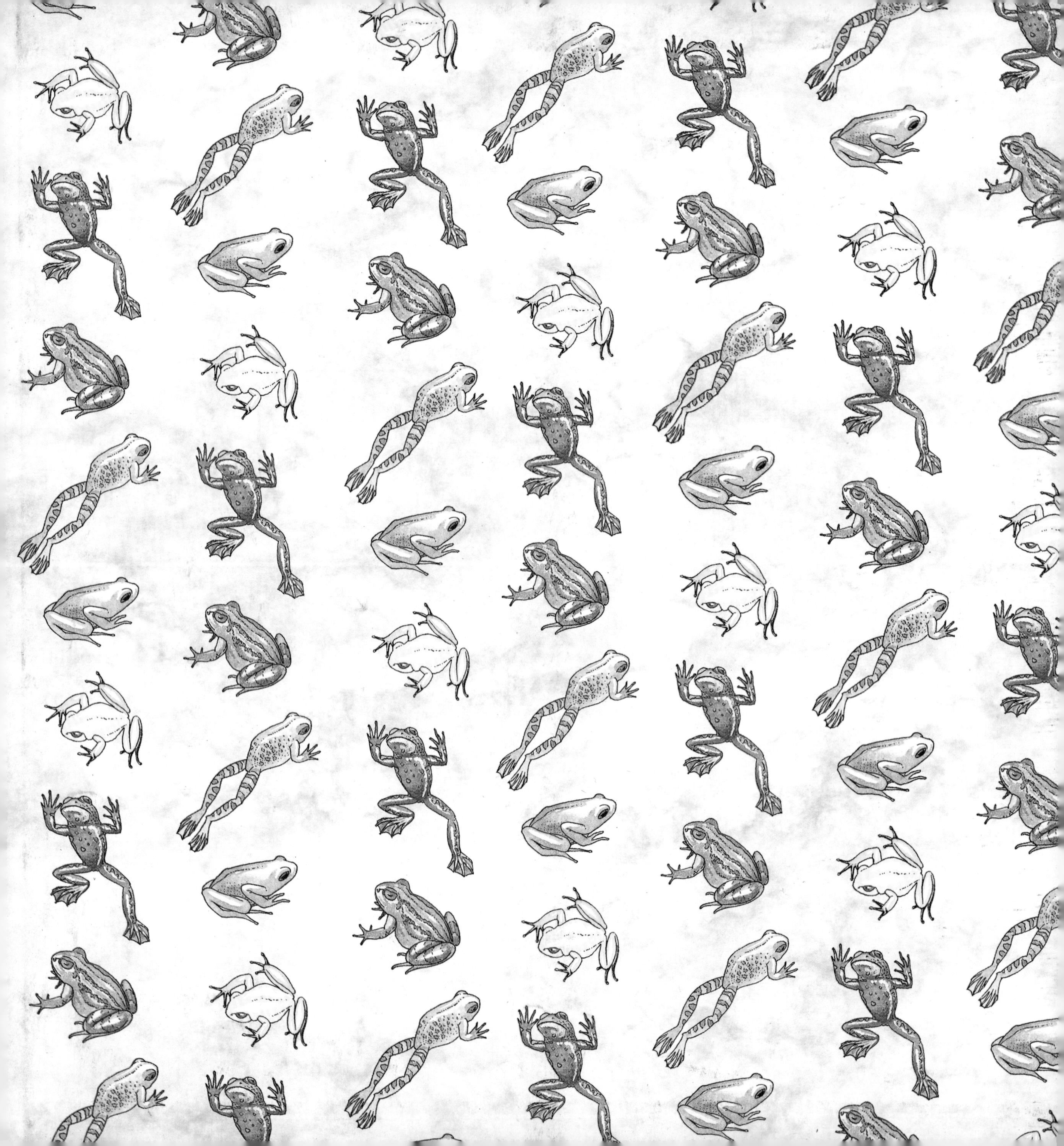